Darnise,

Always remember to use your Playbook
in this game of life!

6-17-23

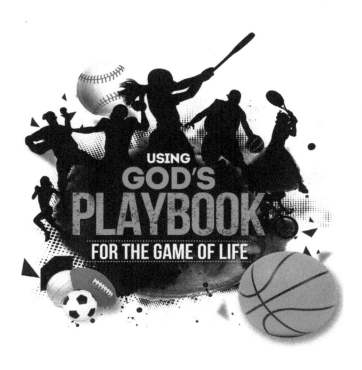

BY:

TONYA MAY AVENT

Vine Publishing's name and logo are trademarks of Vine Publishing, Inc.
ISBN: 978-1-7367483-9-8 (paperback)
ISBN: 979-8-218-04972-0 (e-book)

Library of Congress Cataloging-in-Publication Data
Library of Congress Control Number: 2022914587
Published by Vine Publishing, Inc.
New York, NY
www.vinepublish.com
Printed in the United States of America

I dedicate this book to Kennedi - the one who made me a mother. I pray that as we release you to the world, you have a strong foundation in the Word of God, upon which you can stand firmly on for the rest of your life.

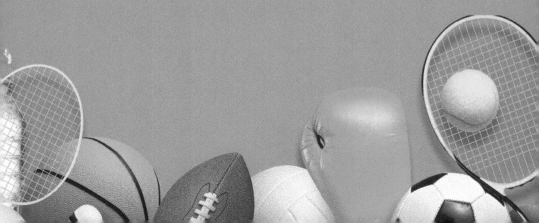

TABLE OF CONTENTS

FROM THE AUTHOR

The summer before she entered high school, my daughter Kennedi experienced a devastating injury while competing to qualify for the USA Track and Field Jr. Olympics. As I was praying for her healing, I was also reciting scriptures I knew that contained God's promises for her future.

Unfortunately, Kennedi did not know many of those scriptures and went through a period of questioning God, wondering why He allowed her to experience such a difficult and painful injury. While I was very strong in my faith due to the scriptures I knew and believed, she was not.

As she recovered, I constantly wondered what would happen once she left for college or was living on her own as an adult and faced a difficult situation or challenge. I wouldn't be around her every day—would she be able to pray for herself and stand on God's Word without my direction?

I realized I had done everything I could to help my daughters be the best athletes they could be—making sure they had the best trainers, played for the best teams, and had the best sports equipment and gear. I had spent more time focused on raising them to be champions, but not nearly as much time teaching them the Word of God.

And it wasn't just us. After years of serving in children's and youth ministry, I realized this was true of countless Christian youth—they just did not have much knowledge of the Bible or a good understanding of its purpose or teachings.

So, I decided to do something about it. I wrote this devotional.

HOW IS THE BIBLE A PLAYBOOK?

As a former athlete, coach's wife, and mother of athletes, I know that playbooks contain important information required for winning. A playbook is a guide that contains strategies, tips, and rules to follow to achieve victory against a challenger or opponent. My family knows all about training and competing to win.

THE HOLY BIBLE IS A TYPE OF PLAYBOOK FOR CHRISTIANS, OR BELIEVERS OF CHRIST, TO USE WHEN FACING DIFFICULT AND TOUGH TIMES IN LIFE.

Each week you will be presented a strategy in the form of a scripture from the Word of God, along with a short devotional on how to relate and apply the strategy to your life.

Each scripture will have seven workouts, one for every day of the week. It's best to find a quiet place to complete it. As part of your exercises, you will have to answer questions and record your thoughts. You will also need to talk to a **Christian** parent, coach, or trusted adult once a week, so think about who you want to be your guide throughout this training. Check off each activity after completing to monitor your progress.

I realize that some of you may think the Bible is boring; however, I can assure you that, even though it's one of the world's oldest books, it is full of amazing stories, miracles, direction, and promises. It is alive with the life-changing promises from God and can be active and powerful if you choose to read and apply it to your life.

Make sure you have a version of the Bible you can understand. You will notice I used multiple versions to make the scripture clearer: New International Version (NIV), New Living Translation (NLT), and New King James Version (NKJV) are the ones I used the most in this book. It's best to try different versions to understand the message better, especially if the message is not clear the first time you read it.

Remember, the goal isn't for you to remember each verse word for word. But you should be able to say each scripture in your own words by the end of each week, understand what it means to you and know how you can use it in your life.

If you faithfully read this devotional and complete all the workouts, in one year your life will look and feel very different than it does right now. As you progress through this book, you will learn about the Father who created you, the Son who died for you, and the Holy Spirit who can help you live the life you were born to live. You will also learn more about yourself and the real-life opponent who works hard every day to defeat you. Finally, you will learn about choices you should make, and the amazing promises you will receive by following your playbook.

All you have to do now is pick a good time to start – New Year's Day, your birthday, the first day of school, the beginning of your sport's season, or any period that signifies a new beginning. You could even start next week. Or today. Tomorrow works too!

ARE YOU READY?
ON YOUR MARK...
GET SET...
LET'S GOOOOOOO!

GUIDE to
USING STRATEGIES

A strategy has been assigned to each weekly scripture. Below you will find the descriptions of each strategy to help you better understand how to use the scripture you are learning each week:

Offensive Strategy

Scriptures that provide a strategy for going on the attack against your opponent.

Defensive Strategy

Scriptures that provide a strategy for defending or avoiding the attack of your opponent.

Formation

Scriptures that give direction for the position you should take to prepare for your opponent's attack.

Trick Play

Scriptures that give direction on thoughts and actions you should take to trick your opponent.

Trap Warning

Scriptures that contain instructions meant to protect you from harmful or dangerous outcomes.

Play Prediction

Scriptures that provide promises that a certain outcome will take place.

Steady State

Scriptures that provide instructions for you to follow regularly for best performance.

Informational

Scriptures that provide general information and knowledge.

Section 1:

WHO IS GOD, THE FATHER?

DARWIN WHO?

In the beginning God created the heavens and the earth.

(Genesis 1:1 NLT)

In science class, you may have learned about the Big Bang theory—the explanation that our world started from a single explosion. Think about our universe – four gas planets and four rocky planets, separated by an asteroid belt, all revolving around a massive sun on different but constant schedules. How could the order of our universe have just suddenly happened from a blast?

The first verse in the Bible explains that all the order and creativity of our universe didn't just happen. Everything we know about our solar system was **intelligently** designed, and not the result of a chance event. All the beauty we see on the earth and when we look up at the sky above is the work of a Creator.

> **WORD FOCUS:**
>
> **Intelligent** - very smart

Trees and plant life awakening in spring after the dead of winter, blooming fully in the summer, only to die again after autumn. For this to repeat year after year doesn't happen by chance; this was specifically designed. The next time you look up to the night sky and see the countless stars, remember that it is all the work of God's hands.

WEEK 1

In the beginning God created the heavens and the earth.

(Genesis 1:1 NLT)

DAY 1: WARM UP

- ☐ Read this week's verse out loud.
- ☐ The "heavens" include the universe surrounding our earth. How do you believe the universe was started?
- ☐ Read the scripture out loud again.
- ☐ Pray that God will show you the truth about how the world was started.

DAY 2: BREAK IT DOWN

- ☐ Read this week's verse out loud.
- ☐ Consider the example in this week's reading: why do you think some parts of the world have the seasons of winter, spring, summer, and fall? Do you think they happen for a purpose?
- ☐ Finish your workout with prayer asking God to help you appreciate the beauty and purpose of His creation.

DAY 3: GET IN POSITION

❏ Read this week's verse out loud.

❏ Note your thoughts about evolution vs creation. Which argument is easier for you to believe after reviewing your thoughts for both?

❏ Repeat the scripture out loud.

❏ Ask God for help with any doubts you may still have about His creation.

DAY 4: HUDDLE UP

❏ Read this week's verse out loud.

❏ Share this week's scripture with your parent, coach, or other trusted adult and ask them to share their thoughts on how and why they believe the earth was created.

❏ Pray together God will help you understand that everything you see was created by Him.

DAY 5: PUSH THROUGH

❏ Try to recite this week's verse out loud without looking.

❏ Spend time thinking about what you have learned and what you were taught about how the world was formed. Write down what you believe to be true.

❏ Recite this week's scripture again.

❏ End by praying that God will help you discuss your view on creation with others.

DAY 6: PRACTICE MAKES PERFECT

❑ Try again to recite this week's verse out loud. Spend time practicing until you can almost say it from memory.

❑ Why do you think the world was created? Do you believe everything was planned and created on purpose, or it just happened? Explain.

❑ Pray that God helps us take care of the earth He blessed us to live on.

DAY 7: FINISH STRONG

❑ Recite this week's verse from memory.

❑ Write down all the amazing things about the universe you can think of. As you go through your list, think about the genius needed to create everything we see and know about the world.

❑ Thank God for being so amazing and creating such a beautiful world for us to live in.

❑ Close out this week by saying the scripture from memory.

MASTERPIECE IN PROGRESS

We are the clay, and you are the potter. We all are formed by your hand. (Isaiah 64:8 NLT)

A potter is an artist who uses their hands to create a work of art from clay. Starting with shapeless material, the potter will have something in mind for the desired creation and will use tools for **molding** and shaping the clay, while cutting off the parts not required for the final masterpiece.

The Creator of our universe is also our Potter. He formed us with His hands on purpose. No one on this earth is an accident. Every part of you was designed by God with a purpose. Each of your muscles and bones was molded specifically to create what you see in the mirror.

Your strength, speed, and flexibility make you different from other athletes. You were designed as one-of-a-kind, but God is not finished with you. You may continue to experience the unpleasant shaping and uncomfortable cutting away of some things keeping you from being

WORD FOCUS:

mold – to shape

the work of art that God had in mind when He started creating you. When you experience painful situations and setbacks, just remember that the Potter is still working on you. Be patient and trust the process. Masterpieces are always worth the wait.

WEEK 2

We are the clay, and you are the potter. We all are formed by your hand. (Isaiah 64:8 NLT)

DAY 1: WARM UP

❏ Read this week's verse out loud.
❏ What does this scripture say about how you were created? What do you think about that?
❏ Read the scripture out loud again.
❏ Pray for God to speak to you this week about how you were formed.

DAY 2: BREAK IT DOWN

❏ Read this week's verse out loud.
❏ Rewrite the scripture in your own words and make it personally about you.
❏ How does a potter form clay? Describe what you think happens when pottery is made. Feel free to look it up if you don't know.
❏ Pray for God to show you what it means to be clay.

DAY 3: GET IN POSITION

❏ Read this week's verse out loud.

- ❑ Think about the different parts that make you up. Write down all the specific and unique things about yourself.
- ❑ Repeat the scripture out loud.
- ❑ Pray for God to show you all the good qualities He gave you when He made you.

DAY 4: HUDDLE UP

- ❑ Read this week's verse out loud.
- ❑ Share this week's scripture with your parent, coach, or other trusted adult and discuss whether you feel you are a mistake or if you were created for a purpose.
- ❑ Pray together that you would realize that you were specifically created by God for a reason.

DAY 5: PUSH THROUGH

- ❑ Try to recite this week's verse out loud without looking.
- ❑ If there is anything you don't like about yourself, tell God about it.
- ❑ Recite this week's scripture again.
- ❑ End by asking God to help you accept yourself exactly how He made you.

DAY 6: PRACTICE MAKES PERFECT

- ❑ Try again to recite this week's verse out loud. Spend time practicing until you can almost say it from memory.
- ❑ Look in the mirror and spend time looking at every part of yourself. No one else has your exact physical or genetic characteristics. Write down why that is important.

❏ Pray that God shows you there is no other person on earth like you.

DAY 7: FINISH STRONG

❏ Recite this week's verse from memory.

❏ Everything about you is unique and special. You have a gift to play your sport, so write down how you can honor God by using your body to always play your best.

❏ Finish your workout with prayer thanking God for being your Potter, and for creating you just the way you are.

ALL YOU'LL EVER NEED

The Lord is my shepherd; I have all that I need.

(Psalms 23:1 NLT)

Sheep are completely **dependent** on a shepherd for all of their needs, especially for food, safety, and guidance. In the Bible times, the shepherd made sure their flock was fed daily, and each evening he counted them and examined them for injuries and disease. He shaved their wool to allow them to maintain their body temperature and move freely. The shepherd also protected the sheep from harm, whether from killers or the environment.

God is our Shepherd and protects us in the same way. He defends us from those who want to harm us. If we are going the wrong way, He pulls us back into safety, even if that changes the plans we make for our life. When things don't always happen how we want them to, we must remember it is because our Shepherd is always protecting us.

> **WORD FOCUS:**
> **dependent** – needing someone else for support

Whenever you feel worried about things you need or the direction your life is going in, think back on this scripture, and remind yourself that you are always being watched and cared for. You may not have everything you want, but you can trust God to provide everything that you will ever need.

WEEK 3

The Lord is my shepherd; I have all that I need.

(Psalms 23:1 NLT)

DAY 1: WARM UP

❑ Read this week's verse out loud.

❑ This is one of the most famous scriptures from the Bible. What does it mean to you, based on the purpose of a shepherd?

❑ Read the scripture out loud again.

❑ Pray for God to speak to you this week about all the ways He cares for you.

DAY 2: BREAK IT DOWN

❑ Read this week's verse out loud.

❑ Rewrite the scripture in your own words and make it personally about you.

❑ Is there anything in your life you need protection from right now?

❑ Pray now to your Shepherd and ask Him to protect you.

DAY 3: GET IN POSITION

❑ Read this week's verse out loud.

❑ Sheep really can't do anything for themselves. What can God as your Shepherd do for you that you can't do for yourself?

❑ Repeat the scripture out loud.

❑ Pray for God to provide the things you need today that you don't currently have.

DAY 4: HUDDLE UP

❑ Read this week's verse out loud.

❑ Discuss a difficult situation (one that requires trust in God) with your parent, coach, or other trusted adult.

❑ Pray together about that situation.

DAY 5: PUSH THROUGH

❑ Try to recite this week's verse out loud without looking.

❑ Shepherds in the Bible used a staff to pull sheep away from the danger they wandered into. Are you on a path you're not supposed to be on? Do you need God to pull you back to safety?

❑ Recite this week's scripture again.

❑ End by praying to God about anything going on in your life that concerns you and ask Him to protect you.

DAY 6: PRACTICE MAKES PERFECT

❑ Try again to recite this week's verse out loud. Spend time practicing until you can almost say it from memory.

❑ Sometimes, the things that are best for us may not always feel good to us. Has this week's lesson shown God's protection for you, even when you didn't know He was being your Shepherd?

❑ Pray that you will always be aware of God's protection at work in your life.

DAY 7: FINISH STRONG

❑ Recite this week's verse. Spend time practicing until you can say it from memory.

❑ You can depend on our Shepherd to provide for and protect you. Write a note to yourself as a reminder that you always have protection. The next time you feel worried, come back to this lesson and scripture as a reminder.

❑ Thank God for always watching over and protecting you.

❑ Close out this week by saying the scripture from memory.

WHOEVER, WHENEVER, WHATEVER & HOWEVER

I AM WHO I AM. (Exodus 3:14 NKJV)

God called Moses to lead his people out of **slavery** in Egypt. Moses was very concerned about what those people would say when he told them that God sent him to save them. He knew they would question him, so he asked God who he should say sent him.

Today's scripture was God's response. God told Moses to tell the people that I AM sent him. This was an extremely powerful statement. God wanted both Moses and the people to know that He was whatever and whoever they needed Him to be for them.

God is still the great I AM today. As humans, we have so many needs, and God can be—or provide—anything we require, at any time. He can help with activities like sports and school. He can help with people like teammates, friends, parents, and siblings. He can help heal physical and emotional injuries. He can help with your future by guiding your college and career choices. And the list goes on and on. No matter what it is, God is whatever we need. There's

> **WORD FOCUS:**
>
> **slavery** – owning another person against their will

nothing we ever have to figure out on our own.

WEEK 4

I AM WHO I AM. (Exodus 3:14 NKJV)

DAY 1: WARM UP

❑ Read this week's verse out loud.

❑ We have discussed God being your Creator, Potter, and Shepherd. Today's scripture gives God more roles. What does this tell you about God?

❑ Read the scripture out loud again.

❑ Pray that this week, God shows you the many roles He can be in your life.

DAY 2: BREAK IT DOWN

❑ Read this week's verse out loud.

❑ Rewrite the scripture in your own words and make it personally about you.

❑ Spend time thinking about anything you may need at this very moment. What do you need God to be for you?

❑ Finish your workout by praying to God about the help you need Him to be for your problem.

DAY 3: GET IN POSITION

❑ Read this week's verse out loud.

- ❑ We can trust God to be what we need in our lives—whether it's a doctor, trainer, friend, coach, or protector. Write down what this means for you.
- ❑ Repeat the scripture out loud.
- ❑ Pray that you will notice God's help in your life.

DAY 4: HUDDLE UP

- ❑ Read this week's verse out loud.
- ❑ Discuss with your parent, coach, or other trusted adult about a situation you could use assistance with, but that they can't provide help for. Determine how God can support you.
- ❑ Pray together that you will trust God to help you with the situation you discussed in your huddle time.

DAY 5: PUSH THROUGH

- ❑ Try to recite this week's verse out loud without looking.
- ❑ Think deeper about everything going on in your life. Do you need help with your family? Is everything going okay in school? Are you or someone you know injured or sick?
- ❑ Recite this week's scripture again.
- ❑ Pray for a situation you never thought about asking God's help for. No matter how big or small it is, God wants you to ask for His assistance.

DAY 6: PRACTICE MAKES PERFECT

- ❑ Try again to recite this week's verse out loud. Spend time practicing until you can almost say it from memory.

- [ ] Do you have a friend or teammate that has a problem or issue? Would you be willing to share this week's lesson with them and ask God to help them?
- [ ] Pray that God would give you the courage to share this message with people you know who need help.

DAY 7: FINISH STRONG

- [ ] Recite this week's verse. Spend time practicing until you can say it from memory.
- [ ] Think about all the different areas where you need help from someone who is bigger, stronger, smarter, or has more resources.
- [ ] Thank God for what you've learned about Him this week, and pray that you would always go to Him first when you have a problem.
- [ ] Close out this week by saying the scripture from memory.

YOU HAVE LIMITLESS POSSIBILITIES

With God everything is possible. (Matthew 19:26 NLT)

In the story of David and Goliath, there was no way that David should have beaten Goliath in battle. Goliath was a giant that everyone feared, while David was just an ordinary young man. But before he threw the stone at Goliath's head, David proclaimed, "*I come to you in the name of the Lord.*" (1 Samuel 17:45)

Because God created everything in this world, He has the power to control everything in it. There is absolutely nothing He can't do. The Bible has countless stories of God doing things that would be impossible for a human to do on their own. We can find many examples that show how mighty and powerful God is.

David vs. Goliath is the ultimate **underdog** story. We even hear the term in the sports world when a smaller challenger or team goes against a seemingly unbeatable opponent. But we've seen it happen time and time again. Goliath comes tumbling down. If you have what seems to be an impossible dream or goal, don't give up. There is

> **WORD FOCUS:**
>
> **underdog** – someone who has a little chance of winning

nothing too hard for God!

WEEK 5

With God everything is possible. (Matthew 19:26 NLT)

DAY 1: WARM UP

❏ Read this week's verse out loud.

❏ Think about this week's scripture. Do you really believe anything is possible with God? Why or why not?

❏ Read the scripture out loud again.

❏ Pray that, this week, God will show you that nothing is impossible for Him.

DAY 2: BREAK IT DOWN

❏ Read this week's verse out loud.

❏ Rewrite the scripture in your own words and make it personally about you.

❏ God did the impossible many times in the Bible: healing people, raising them from the dead, and allowing older people to have children. Do you think those kinds of things are possible today?

❏ Finish your workout by praying that God would increase your confidence in Him.

DAY 3: GET IN POSITION

- ❑ Read this week's verse out loud.
- ❑ What could change about your life if you knew there was nothing you couldn't accomplish with God?
- ❑ Repeat the scripture out loud.
- ❑ Pray that God will give you the faith and confidence needed to believe Him for anything.

DAY 4: HUDDLE UP

- ❑ Read this week's verse out loud.
- ❑ Discuss with your parent, coach, or other trusted adult about what you would like to happen but seems impossible for your life.
- ❑ Share the verse you are learning this week and ask for their thoughts.
- ❑ Pray together that you would believe God to do what seems impossible in your life.

DAY 5: PUSH THROUGH

- ❑ Try to recite this week's verse out loud without looking.
- ❑ Are there any limits that you've put on yourself without realizing it? Is there something you want to do or have happen, but gave up because you felt it was too impossible to happen?
- ❑ Recite this week's scripture again.
- ❑ End by praying that God will give you hope as you pray and believe for Him to do impossible things in your life.

DAY 6: PRACTICE MAKES PERFECT

❑ Try again to recite this week's verse out loud. Spend time practicing until you can almost say it from memory.

❑ Think about the things you prayed for this week. What is the reason you want God to do them for you? Realize that God won't always answer everything you pray for, as it should be something that brings Him glory. How does what you need bring Him glory?

❑ Pray that you will understand why you are asking for God to answer your prayer, and that your prayers will always be for His glory.

DAY 7: FINISH STRONG

❑ Recite this week's verse. Spend time practicing until you can say it from memory.

❑ There is nothing too big for you to dream for, hope for, or pray for. The great I AM that we learned about last week has unlimited power.

❑ Pray that God will take any limits off your prayers and that you would believe God for anything you need.

❑ Close out this week by saying the scripture from memory.

Section 2:

WHO IS JESUS?

BEST. GIFT. EVER.

For God loved the world so much that he gave his only Son, so that everyone who believes in him may not die but have eternal life.

(John 3:16 GNB)

When Tim Tebow played football for the University of Florida, he wore John 3:16 written on his under-eye blacks during the 2009 Championship game. Millions of people googled the verse, and it became one of the biggest searched phrases ever. If you've ever watched any major sporting event on TV, there is usually a sign in the crowd with this famous verse on it.

Since we are **sinners** from birth, there is nothing we can do to get rid of it. No matter how hard we try to live a perfect life, we will never be able to. So, God sent His only Son Jesus to earth, as the solution to this human problem. Because Jesus is God's Son, He was not born with the same sinful human nature as the rest of mankind.

> **WORD FOCUS:**
>
> **sinner** – someone who has broken God's law or rules

Being sinless, Jesus paid the price to cover our sins by dying on the cross. No event in history has ever topped that—not walking on the moon, not curing a disease, not winning a World Championship or an MVP award. This act of love has changed the future of every person who believes in Jesus.

WEEK 6

For God loved the world so much that he gave his only Son, so that everyone who believes in him may not die but have eternal life.
(John 3:16 GNB)

DAY 1: WARM UP

❑ Read this week's verse out loud.

❑ Did you know that Jesus died for you? How does it make you feel to know that He died because of the sin in your life?

❑ Read the scripture out loud again.

❑ Pray for God to speak to you this week about His amazing love for you.

DAY 2: BREAK IT DOWN

❑ Read this week's verse out loud.

❑ Rewrite the scripture in your own words and make it personally about you.

❑ As the Son of God, Jesus was not born with the same sinful nature as every human that has ever been born. His spiritual DNA allowed His death on the cross to keep us from being separated from God forever.

❑ Finish your workout with prayer, thanking God for His plan to always keep you connected to Him.

DAY 3: GET IN POSITION

❑ Read this week's verse out loud.

❑ When Jesus died on the cross, His death paid the price for our sins. What does this scripture tell you about love?

❑ Repeat the scripture out loud.

❑ Thank God for His love that made him give up His son, and thank Jesus for giving up His life, just for you.

DAY 4: HUDDLE UP

❑ Read this week's verse out loud.

❑ Discuss with your parent, coach, or other trusted adult about what Jesus dying on the cross means to them. Also, discuss what it means to have eternal life.

❑ Share the verse you are learning this week and ask for their thoughts.

❑ Pray together, thanking God for His plan to free you from sin and allow you to live with Him forever.

DAY 5: PUSH THROUGH

❑ Try to recite this week's verse out loud without looking.

❑ If we believe in Jesus, this scripture says we will not die but have eternal life. This does not mean we won't have a human death, but it does mean we won't have a spiritual death, so we will live forever in heaven with God. What does it mean to die on earth, but to live in heaven?

❑ Recite this week's scripture again.

❑ End by asking God to help you understand that human death is not the end for Believers, and thank Him for eternal life.

DAY 6: PRACTICE MAKES PERFECT

❑ Try again to recite this week's verse out loud. Spend time practicing until you can almost say it from memory.

❑ If you believe that Jesus was sent to earth to die for you, and to free you from the sin you were born with, you can ask Him into your life to save you and guide you forever. This single act of believing and confessing is what allows us to live forever. Do you truly believe that Jesus died for you?

❑ Thank Jesus for His ultimate sacrifice of giving up his life so you would be free from sin and can now live forever.

DAY 7: FINISH STRONG

❑ Recite this week's verse. Spend time practicing until you can say it from memory.

❑ John 3:16 is the most important scripture in this book, as it is the foundation for the gospel or good news about Jesus Christ. The gospel is that God gave His only Son, Jesus, as a gift to all of mankind, so sin would not keep us separated, but that after we die on earth, we would live in heaven. If you have never asked Jesus to live in your heart, consider praying the sinner's prayer found at the end of this book so you can have endless life with Him.

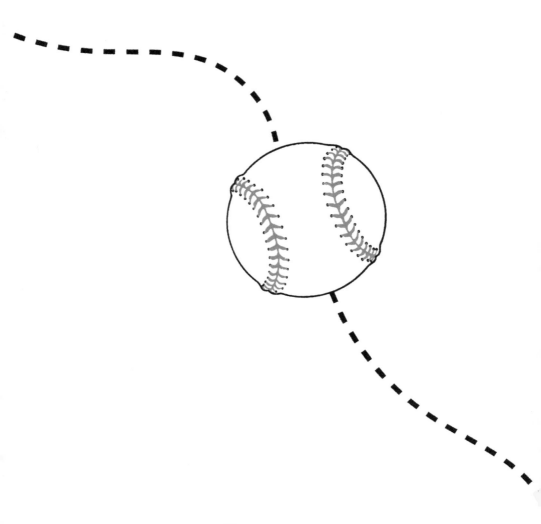

THE GIFT THAT KEEPS ON GIVING

Christ died for our sins according to the Scriptures, and that He was buried, and that He rose again the third day according to the Scriptures. (1 Corinthians 15:3-4 NKJV)

As we celebrate Jesus' birth during the Christmas season, we give presents to **symbolize** His life-changing gift to this world. A few months later, we reflect on the ultimate **sacrifice** of His death on Good Friday and then rejoice on Easter as we celebrate the victory gained when He woke up from His grave.

Jesus willingly endured so much pain leading up to His death and gave up His life just for us. It's the reason He was born. The beauty of this story is that it didn't end when He died. When Jesus woke up three days later, He overpowered all of the sin in the world—including yours and mine.

> **WORD FOCUS:**
>
> **symbolize** – to represent or stand for something else
>
> **sacrifice** – to suffer or give up something for someone else

We are not perfect and may not always feel worthy of that kind of love, but it doesn't matter to Jesus. He still loves us and would have still died the same way if we were the only people in the world. There's no gift that anyone could ever give us that would be greater than that.

WEEK 7

Christ died for our sins according to the Scriptures, and that He was buried, and that He rose again the third day according to the Scriptures. (1 Corinthians 15:3-4 NKJV)

DAY 1: WARM UP
- ❏ Read this week's verse out loud.
- ❏ God gave His Son to save the world from sin. Do you think Jesus dying for your sin was fair?
- ❏ Read the scripture out loud again.
- ❏ Pray that you would understand how great the gift of Jesus is to your life.

DAY 2: BREAK IT DOWN
- ❏ Read this week's verse out loud.
- ❏ Rewrite the scripture in your own words and make it personally about you.
- ❏ Jesus knew He had to die to save us. How would it feel knowing the only reason you were born was to die, to help someone else?
- ❏ Pray that you would never forget to be thankful for the gift

of Jesus in your life.

DAY 3: GET IN POSITION

- ❏ Read this week's verse out loud.
- ❏ What do you think would have happened if Jesus didn't die for you? What does His gift mean for your life?
- ❏ Repeat the scripture out loud.
- ❏ Pray that you understand the future you were saved from after Jesus rose from His grave.

DAY 4: HUDDLE UP

- ❏ Read this week's verse out loud.
- ❏ Discuss with your parent, coach, or other trusted adult the importance of Jesus dying, being buried, and then rising from the dead. Do you feel worthy of that kind of love?
- ❏ Share the verse you are learning this week and ask for their thoughts.
- ❏ Pray together, thanking Jesus for loving you enough to die for you.

DAY 5: PUSH THROUGH

- ❏ Try to recite this week's verse out loud without looking.
- ❏ When Jesus died, He was whipped and beaten for hours. Nails were driven into his hands and feet, to hang Him on a cross in agony until He finally died. Why do you think He experienced a violent death while trying to save us?
- ❏ Recite this week's scripture again.
- ❏ End today by thanking Jesus for all He endured leading up

to His death, so He could save you from your sin.

DAY 6: PRACTICE MAKES PERFECT

- ❏ Try again to recite this week's verse out loud. Spend time practicing until you can almost say it from memory.
- ❏ Jesus dying on the cross, being buried, and then rising again is the most meaningful event that has ever happened to mankind. Its impact will last forever and ever. How will this gift change your future?
- ❏ Thank God for giving you the gift of eternal life through Jesus Christ.

DAY 7: FINISH STRONG

- ❏ Recite this week's verse. Spend time practicing until you can say it from memory.
- ❏ Is there anyone you would die for? How much love would cause someone to give up their life for another? What does it mean to have someone do that for you?
- ❏ Pray that God will help you always appreciate the most amazing gift you have ever received, and that He would help you tell others that they have the same gift.
- ❏ Close out this week by saying the scripture from memory.

A BRAND-NEW LIFE

This means that anyone who belongs to Christ has become a new person. The old life is gone; a new life has begun!

(2 Corinthians 5:17 NLT)

Think about a movie you saw or a book you read about a person who acted one way at the start of the story, but after certain events happened, that person's behavior changed. Usually, something happens that affects the character deeply, who then changes their behavior, much to the surprise of everyone that knew the "old" version of them. The story usually ends with signs that a better future is ahead because of the change.

We experience that same change when we ask Jesus into our lives. We receive **eternal** life when Jesus lives in our hearts, meaning that after we die on earth, we will live with

> **WORD FOCUS:**
>
> **eternal** – to last forever
>
> **gradual** – moving or changing slowly

Him in heaven forever. We receive the gift of forgiveness since we were born into a life of sin. Through forgiveness from Jesus, we are free from the guilt of our past mistakes and bad choices.

When we understand these changes that come from giving

ourselves to Christ, it leads to a new life. Inviting Jesus into our lives will help us think, talk and act differently than we have in the past. For some, that change is immediate. For others, it may be **gradual**, starting with reading the Bible, attending church, and getting to know more about God. Once the change starts, people will notice!

WEEK 8

This means that anyone who belongs to Christ has become a new person. The old life is gone; a new life has begun!

(2 Corinthians 5:17 NLT)

DAY 1: WARM UP
- ❑ Read this week's verse out loud.
- ❑ Are there any changes you want to make in your life?
- ❑ Read the scripture out loud again.
- ❑ Pray for God to speak to you this week about becoming a new person.

DAY 2: BREAK IT DOWN
- ❑ Read this week's verse out loud.
- ❑ Rewrite the scripture in your own words and make it personally about you.

- Have you ever noticed a difference in a friend or teammate's behavior? Did you ever wonder what caused it? Did you ask?
- Pray that Jesus would show you how your life can be different with Him.

DAY 3: GET IN POSITION

- Read this week's verse out loud.
- Are there things in your life you have been trying to change on your own? Maybe your attitude, your dedication to practice, or your study habits. How successful were you without help?
- Repeat the scripture out loud.
- Ask Jesus to make you aware of all the changes He is making in your life.

DAY 4: HUDDLE UP

- Read this week's verse out loud.
- Discuss with your parent, coach, or other trusted adult about changes Jesus has made since He came into their life. What did you learn during this discussion?
- Share the verse you are learning this week and ask for their thoughts.
- Pray together that Jesus would continue to change you both into new people.

DAY 5: PUSH THROUGH

- Try to recite this week's verse out loud without looking.

- What do you think it means to become a new person? Are there things you don't want to change in your life? What are they?
- Recite this week's scripture again.
- End by asking Jesus to help you let go of any thoughts or behavior that do not please Him.

DAY 6: PRACTICE MAKES PERFECT

- Try again to recite this week's verse out loud. Spend time practicing until you can almost say it from memory.
- Identify those things in your life that you know Jesus wants to change. Write down ways you will commit to changing the things on your list.
- Pray that Jesus will continue to help you identify anything in your life that needs to change.

DAY 7: FINISH STRONG

- Recite this week's verse. Spend time practicing until you can say it from memory.
- Have you asked Jesus into your heart? If so, what changes have you experienced as a result? If not, would you like to say the prayer found in the back of this book?
- Thank God for bringing change into your life and removing the things that do not belong.
- Close out this week by saying the scripture from memory.

FRUIT

I am the vine; you are the branches. Those who remain in me, and I in them, will produce much fruit. (John 15:5a NLT)

A tomato plant's vines grow upward, and the branches grow off the vine. As the branches are fed from the vine, tomatoes **sprout** from them. The plant requires both sunshine and rain as it grows. The health of the tomato depends on the branch's connection to the vine. If the branch is somehow separated from the vine, or if all the **nutrients** are not getting through, the branch will not produce healthy tomatoes.

Jesus is the vine for Christians. Because He lives inside us, we begin to grow and produce fruit with our actions. This growth comes through praying, reading our Bible, and learning more about Him. And just like the vine produces tomatoes, Jesus' influence causes us to bear fruit, which are positive words and actions that other people can benefit from.

> **WORD FOCUS:**
>
> **sprout** – to grow
>
> **nutrients** – something needed to make something else grow and be healthy

We should want to live in a way that always produces fruit.

Be careful not to miss spending time with Jesus. When we are not connected to Him, we will stop bearing fruit. Also watch out for bad influences in your life, as it can cause you to produce rotten fruit, which may harm others. Stay close to Jesus every day so you can always produce good fruit.

WEEK 9

I am the vine; you are the branches. Those who remain in me, and I in them, will produce much fruit. (John 15:5a NLT)

DAY 1: WARM UP

- ❏ Read this week's verse out loud.
- ❏ Are you connected to Jesus? If so, how are you producing fruit?
- ❏ Read the scripture out loud again.
- ❏ Pray for God to show you how to produce more fruit in your life.

DAY 2: BREAK IT DOWN

- ❏ Read this week's verse out loud.
- ❏ Rewrite the scripture in your own words and make it personally about you.
- ❏ What are you doing to grow spiritually? Are you reading your Bible and studying your devotionals every day, or do

you skip some days?

❑ Finish your workout asking Jesus to help you stay dedicated to reading your Bible and learning more about Him.

DAY 3: GET IN POSITION

❑ Read this week's verse out loud.

❑ Are there difficult situations going on in your life? Maybe that major disappointment, injury, or setback is a storm to help you grow and bear more fruit. What do you think is the purpose of your tough situations?

❑ Repeat the scripture out loud.

❑ Ask God for help in completing this step.

DAY 4: HUDDLE UP

❑ Read this week's verse out loud.

❑ Discuss with your parent, coach, or other trusted adult about the fruit they are producing in their lives from being connected to Jesus. Discuss how they manage to stay connected as busy adults.

❑ Share the verse you are learning this week and ask for their thoughts.

❑ Pray together that you stay connected to Jesus, the vine.

DAY 5: PUSH THROUGH

❑ Try to recite this week's verse out loud without looking.

❑ Think about those that are close to you, that may not be a good influence. How are your words and behavior around them? What do you think you should do?

- ❑ Recite this week's scripture again.
- ❑ End by praying that Jesus would help you cut out anything or anyone that has caused you to produce rotten fruit.

DAY 6: PRACTICE MAKES PERFECT

- ❑ Try again to recite this week's verse out loud. Spend time practicing until you can almost say it from memory.
- ❑ Think about ways you can continue to produce fruit. Write down areas you will commit to focus on, like regularly reading your Bible, attending church, hanging out with other Believers, and spending one-on-one time with God.
- ❑ Pray for help as you commit to finding ways to connect to Jesus, the vine.

DAY 7: FINISH STRONG

- ❑ Recite this week's verse. Spend time practicing until you can say it from memory.
- ❑ Write down what would be different if you allowed Jesus to influence your thoughts, choices, and actions.
- ❑ Pray that you will remain in Jesus and He would remain in you so you will always produce fruit that will honor Him and benefit others.
- ❑ Close out this week by saying the scripture from memory.

LIVING YOUR BEST LIFE

I have come that they may have life, and that they may have it more **abundantly.** (John 10:10b NKJV)

The phone was invented for two people to talk while in separate locations. Over the years, however, it evolved into a smartphone, which has more purposes. You can text, email, video chat, surf the web, watch videos, and play games. The phone has definitely advanced from its original purpose, and there are countless ways it can be used.

Jesus came to earth to save the world from our sins. However, during his life, He did more than that. While living He taught people about God, and performed miracles like healing the sick and raising the dead to life again. Jesus often helped the people He came across; it didn't matter if they needed physical, emotional, or spiritual assistance. He wanted them to live a full life.

> **WORD FOCUS:**
> **abundantly** – in large amounts

Jesus is still helping us today. We don't ever have to struggle at a lower level than He created for us. Are there some areas of your life—like grades, friendships, athletic performances, or family relationships—that are not at their fullest level? Ask God to help you give your best every day, accomplish all you can, and make an impact on the world. Otherwise, it's like you're an old phone. Time for an upgrade!

WEEK 10

I have come that they may have life, and that they may have it more abundantly. (John 10:10b NKJV)

DAY 1: WARM UP

- ❏ Read this week's verse out loud.
- ❏ Think about the word 'abundant'. What do you think an abundant life looks like?
- ❏ Read the scripture out loud again.
- ❏ Pray for Jesus to help you understand how He wants to do great things in your life.

DAY 2: BREAK IT DOWN

- ❏ Read this week's verse out loud.
- ❏ Rewrite the scripture in your own words and make it personally about you.
- ❏ Have you ever received a gift that has more than one purpose? Something that had a main feature but did other things as well? Did that help you appreciate the gift and use it more?

❑ Finish your workout by praying that you would open your life to endless possibilities of doing things for Jesus.

DAY 3: GET IN POSITION

❑ Read this week's verse out loud.
❑ Do you have any relationships beneath where they should be? What can you do to ensure you are living at the level God wants you to live at?
❑ Repeat the scripture out loud.
❑ Ask Jesus to show you anything or anyone in your life that may be keeping you at a lower level than you are supposed to be at right now.

DAY 4: HUDDLE UP

❑ Read this week's verse out loud.
❑ Discuss with your parent, coach, or other trusted adult, the different ways you can do more with your life to make a difference. Discuss if there are books, training, or mentoring that will provide helpful information.
❑ Share the verse you are learning this week and ask for their thoughts.
❑ Pray together that Jesus will show you the different ways He can use your life for His glory.

DAY 5: PUSH THROUGH

❑ Try to recite this week's verse out loud without looking.
❑ Jesus was the most important and impactful person who ever lived. He originally came to earth to die for our sins,

but He did so much more like healing people and giving them hope. How can He use your life in different ways to touch someone else?

❑ Recite this week's scripture again.

❑ End by praying that you will have the courage to make a difference in someone else's life.

DAY 6: PRACTICE MAKES PERFECT

❑ Try again to recite this week's verse out loud. Spend time practicing until you can almost say it from memory.

❑ We have reviewed the many benefits of the gifts we were given through the life of Jesus Christ. Is there any area of your life you're not happy with that you'd like Jesus to help you improve?

❑ Pray and give Jesus every area of your life you want His help with.

DAY 7: FINISH STRONG

❑ Recite this week's verse. Spend time practicing until you can say it from memory.

❑ When Jesus came to earth, nothing He did was to benefit himself. His purpose was always to die for us. But He left His mark on the world by changing the lives of the people He met wherever He went.

❑ Thank Jesus for changing the course of history by coming to earth, and pray that you will also make an impact on the people who come into your life now and in the future.

❏ Close out this week by saying the scripture from memory.

Section 3:

WHO IS THE HOLY SPIRIT?

A NEW FRIEND

And I will pray the Father, and he will give you another Counselor to be with you for ever. (John 14:16 RSV)

Jesus and His twelve disciples were a tight group. Imagine Jesus as the team captain who led for three years. He taught the disciples many things, and they saw Him perform miracle after miracle. Jesus knew He was going to die and had to prepare them to go on without Him. He assured them that after He died, God would send them another **companion** to counsel, help, and guide them; one who would never leave them.

That Counselor is the Holy Spirit, the invisible presence of God, who dwells inside us from the moment we believe in Jesus Christ and accept Him as our Savior. In the same way we cannot see the wind but feel it on our skin when it blows, we may feel the Holy Spirit inside of us. Our minds can understand His voice, even though no one around us may be aware.

> **WORD FOCUS:**
>
> **companion** — a person to spend a lot of time with

We can grow our relationship with the Holy Spirit through prayer, reading our Bible and other Bible-based books, and learning more about God through sermons or messages spoken at our local church or online. We start to feel and hear Him as we continue to develop a relationship with Him.

WEEK 11

And I will pray the Father, and he will give you another Counselor to be with you for ever. (John 14:16 RSV)

DAY 1: WARM UP

❏ Read this week's verse out loud.

❏ This week, we learn about the Holy Spirit, who is God's invisible spirit that lives inside us. Verse 17 says people will not accept the Holy Spirit because they can't see Him. Do you have a hard time believing in someone you can't see? Why or why not?

❏ Read the scripture out loud again.

❏ Pray for God to help you understand who the Holy Spirit is this week as you go through your workout.

DAY 2: BREAK IT DOWN

❏ Read this week's verse out loud.

❏ Rewrite the scripture in your own words and make it personally about you.

❏ Multiple versions of the Bible use other words for the Holy Spirit in this verse. Another word used is Companion. Jesus promised the disciples that the Holy Spirit would take His place in their lives after He returned to heaven. Have you ever had an important person suddenly leave your life? Was someone else able to take their place?

❏ Pray that God will show you that you are never alone because the Holy Spirit is always your Companion.

DAY 3: GET IN POSITION

❏ Read this week's verse out loud.

❏ As we continue to examine this verse, we see Jesus uses the word "another". Jesus knew He couldn't be with the disciples forever, so He assured them that another Helper was coming, that would live with them forever. The Holy Spirit is inside of you, to be your Helper, Counselor, and Companion. In what areas in your life do you need help? Do you need someone to talk to about certain things?

❏ Repeat the scripture out loud.

❏ Ask God to show you how to develop a relationship with the Holy Spirit.

DAY 4: HUDDLE UP

❏ Read this week's verse out loud.

❏ Discuss with your parent, coach, or other trusted adult what they know about the Holy Spirit. Ask any questions you may still have about why the Holy Spirit is in your life.

❏ Share the verse you are learning this week and ask for their thoughts.

- ❏ Pray together that you would understand the Holy Spirit's role in your life.

DAY 5: PUSH THROUGH

- ❏ Try to recite this week's verse out loud without looking.
- ❏ Another version of this scripture calls the Holy Spirit a Comforter. Jesus knew the disciples would need comfort after He left them to return to heaven. Have you lost something or someone and need comfort from the Holy Spirit?
- ❏ Recite this week's scripture again.
- ❏ Pray that the Holy Spirit will also be a Comforter to you in those areas where you may have emotional pain.

DAY 6: PRACTICE MAKES PERFECT

- ❏ Try again to recite this week's verse out loud. Spend time practicing until you can almost say it from memory.
- ❏ For the Holy Spirit to be a Companion and Counselor to you, you would have to have a relationship. If there was a new member of your team, a new neighbor on your block, or a new classmate at school, how would you build a relationship and get to know them better? Can you follow the same example while getting to know the Holy Spirit?
- ❏ Pray that God would allow you to feel the Holy Spirit inside of you.

DAY 7: FINISH STRONG

- ❏ Recite this week's verse. Spend time practicing until you

can say it from memory.

❑ How does it feel to know God's Spirit is living inside of you? Do you ever hear Him talking to you? If you are not a Believer, consider saying the prayer in the back of this book and asking Jesus to live in your heart, so the Holy Spirit will also come and live inside you, and be your Companion and Helper forever.

❑ Pray that you would be able to hear the Holy Spirit communicating with you and that you would build a relationship with Him.

❑ Close out this week by saying the scripture from memory.

NOTHING BUT THE TRUTH

When the Spirit of truth comes, he will guide you into all truth.

(John 16:13 NLT)

The Jungle Book is a story about a boy named Mowgli who was raised by wolves. He hunted like a wolf, ate like a wolf, and even walked on his hands and feet. He believed he was a wolf until he met a human. Then his **perspective** about who he was changed.

A person's truth may be based on their beliefs, how they were raised, and how they see the world. However, once new information is received, understanding and beliefs can change. The Holy Spirit is our guide to learning the truth. He helps us separate what is true from what is false.

The Bible contains the truth about who we are and the promises God has given us when we follow His Word. Some things you may learn while reading this devotional may be different

WORD FOCUS:

perspective – view about something

from what you previously believed. But if God's Word says it, then it is true, and nothing can change that. Not what your friends believe, or what your teacher says, or even what society thinks. If you follow what you learn from God's Spirit as you read your Bible, then you'll always walk in the truth.

When the Spirit of truth comes, he will guide you into all truth.

(John 16:13 NLT)

DAY 1: WARM UP

❑ Read this week's verse out loud.

❑ What do you use to determine if something is real or fake? How do you know the truth from a lie?

❑ Read the scripture out loud again.

❑ Pray that the Holy Spirit will show you how to determine the truth in your life.

DAY 2: BREAK IT DOWN

❑ Read this week's verse out loud.

❑ Rewrite the scripture in your own words and make it personally about you.

❑ If there is something you've always believed to be true, are you open to changing your mind? What would you do if you learned new information?

❑ Pray that the Holy Spirit would help you be open to any new information you learn this week and for the rest of this devotional.

DAY 3: GET IN POSITION

❑ Read this week's verse out loud.

❑ There may be times we believe things our friends, family, coaches, teammates, and society tell us about ourselves, that we know deep down are not true. How do you think the Holy Spirit can help you respond when that happens?

❑ Repeat the scripture out loud.

❑ Pray that the Holy Spirit will show you everything true and not true about you so you don't believe lies about yourself.

DAY 4: HUDDLE UP

❑ Read this week's verse out loud.

❑ Discuss with your parent, coach, or other trusted adult about their definition of the truth, and how the Holy Spirit helps them understand what they read in the Bible.

❑ Share the verse you are learning this week and ask for their thoughts.

❑ Pray that you would fully understand the role the Holy Spirit should have in your life.

DAY 5: PUSH THROUGH

❑ Try to recite this week's verse out loud without looking.

❑ There may be times when we are the ones telling ourselves something that isn't true. Do you ever tell yourself you're not smart enough, not athletic enough, not talented enough, or that you can't do something? Where do you think this judgment comes from?

- ❏ Recite this week's scripture again.
- ❏ End today's workout by praying that you will never speak down to yourself or believe negative things about yourself.

DAY 6: PRACTICE MAKES PERFECT

- ❏ Try again to recite this week's verse out loud. Spend time practicing until you can almost say it from memory.
- ❏ Technology today allows us to find information about any subject in a matter of seconds. This information can easily be shared, even if it has not been verified to be true. How can the sharing of false information so easily impact what people believe?
- ❏ Pray that you will not believe everything you read or see online without verifying it through the knowledge the Holy Spirit has given you.

DAY 7: FINISH STRONG

- ❏ Recite this week's verse. Spend time practicing until you can say it from memory.
- ❏ When you get further in this devotional, you will learn promises that may not currently be happening in your life right now, but they are still true about your future. As you learn the truth about who you are, and God's promises for you, don't ever let anyone or anything allow you to believe otherwise.
- ❏ Pray that the Holy Spirit helps you to continue to read your Bible so you can stay on the path to truth.

❏ Close out this week by saying the scripture from memory.

A VOICE WHEN YOU NEED IT

The Holy Spirit helps us in our weakness. For example, we don't know what God wants us to pray for. But the Holy Spirit prays for us with groanings that cannot be expressed in words.

(Romans 8:26 NLT)

We all have struggles and weaknesses. Maybe you struggle with being truthful. Or you might take things that don't belong to you. Or you might tend to bully a classmate, teammate, or sibling. There may be times when we feel so helpless about our problems that we don't know what to say or think about them.

We are not alone in our efforts to overcome the tough challenges in our lives. This is where the Holy Spirit steps in. When you find yourself in a situation and you're not quite sure how to pray, the Holy Spirit knows exactly how to pray for you. When you're too upset to even talk, just groan or moan what you're feeling, and allow the Holy Spirit to pray through your unspoken sounds.

WORD FOCUS:

ashamed – to feel embarrassed

We don't have to solve our problems on our own. There are times when we don't know how to pray for help concerning those things we are struggling with. We don't always know the right words, or maybe we do but feel too **ashamed** to talk to God about it. Trust that the Holy Spirit knows what you need, and He'll pray for you with all the right words until you can pray on your own again.

WEEK 13

The Holy Spirit helps us in our weakness. For example, we don't know what God wants us to pray for. But the Holy Spirit prays for us with groanings that cannot be expressed in words.

(Romans 8:26 NLT)

DAY 1: WARM UP

❏ Read this week's verse out loud.

❏ Have you ever been so upset you couldn't talk? How do you communicate when you're not able to speak?

❏ Read the scripture out loud again.

❏ Pray that you will understand how and why the Holy Spirit prays for you.

DAY 2: BREAK IT DOWN

❏ Read this week's verse out loud.

❏ Rewrite the scripture in your own words and make it personally about you.

❏ Has anyone ever prayed for you? Do you know what they

prayed for? Did God answer their prayer?

- ❏ Thank God for putting people in your life that pray for you.

DAY 3: GET IN POSITION

- ❏ Read this week's verse out loud.
- ❏ How does it feel to know the Holy Spirit is praying for you and knows all of your weaknesses?
- ❏ Repeat the scripture out loud.
- ❏ Pray that you will trust the Holy Spirit as He prays for you.

DAY 4: HUDDLE UP

- ❏ Read this week's verse out loud.
- ❏ Discuss with your parent, coach, or other trusted adult about intercession (praying for someone else). Why is it important to pray for others?
- ❏ Pray together that as the Holy Spirit prays for you, you will also pray for others.

DAY 5: PUSH THROUGH

- ❏ Try to recite this week's verse out loud without looking.
- ❏ The Holy Spirit always knows what God's will is for you, so His prayers always get answered. What do you think the Holy Spirit is praying to happen in your life right now?
- ❏ Recite this week's scripture again.
- ❏ Thank the Holy Spirit for praying that God's will is done in your life, even though you may not know what God's will is right now.

DAY 6: PRACTICE MAKES PERFECT

❑ Try again to recite this week's verse out loud. Spend time practicing until you can almost say it from memory.

❑ How do you think the Holy Spirit communicates with God through groans? How do you think they understand each other?

❑ Pray that you would always allow the Holy Spirit to pray through your voice.

DAY 7: FINISH STRONG

❑ Recite this week's verse. Spend time practicing until you can say it from memory.

❑ When you have a problem but don't know what to pray for, the Holy Spirit is always available to pray for you, but not in a way you can understand. Can you trust the Holy Spirit's prayers for you? Why or Why not?

❑ Thank the Holy Spirit for praying for the areas in your life you need the most help with. Also thank God for always answering the Holy Spirit's prayers about you.

❑ Close out this week by saying the scripture from memory.

ALWAYS ON YOUR SIDE

But the Advocate, the Holy Spirit, whom the Father will send in my name, will teach you all things and remind you of everything I have said to you. (John 14:26 NIV)

An **advocate** is one of the most important things you can have in your life, as they support a cause or action that improves your life. Coaches advocate by supporting the progress and improvement of their athletes. Parents advocate for their child's education, physical, emotional, and mental health. An advocate supports with things you probably can't accomplish on your own.

God knew we would need help after Jesus left the earth, so He sent the Holy Spirit to be our Advocate. Also referred to as a Helper, the Holy Spirit can assist in any area of our lives. He will help you remember what you have learned in this book, along with what you've ever been taught at home and church. He will let you know the best decision to make when you are faced with a problem and can teach you all that God wants you to know to live a full life.

> **WORD FOCUS:**
>
> **advocate** – one who supports or defends a person or cause

When you find yourself in a tough situation and need

assistance, remember you have help, as the Holy Spirit is always available. You'll never have to figure out or face anything on your own again. You have all the support you'll ever need in the Holy Spirit.

WEEK 14

But the Advocate, the Holy Spirit, whom the Father will send in my name, will teach you all things and remind you of everything I have said to you. (John 14:26 NIV)

DAY 1: WARM UP

❑ Read this week's verse out loud.

❑ Think about the different people in your life that help you do things you can't do on your own. What are some ways they have helped you?

❑ Read the scripture out loud again.

❑ Pray that you would understand all the ways the Holy Spirit advocates for you, by helping you know or get what you need in your life.

DAY 2: BREAK IT DOWN

❑ Read this week's verse out loud.

❑ Rewrite the scripture in your own words and make it personally about you.

- Jesus spent three years teaching His disciples. The Holy Spirit continued teaching them after Jesus went to heaven. Write down all the people who have taught you something about God.
- Thank God for all the people in your life who have taught you about Him.

DAY 3: GET IN POSITION

- Read this week's verse out loud.
- Just as the Holy Spirit taught the disciples, He continues to teach us today. How have you been taught about living as a Christian? In what ways have you learned about God?
- Repeat the scripture out loud.
- Pray that you will continue to grow spiritually as the Holy Spirit teaches you.

DAY 4: HUDDLE UP

- Read this week's verse out loud.
- Discuss with your parent, coach, or other trusted adult about how they advocate for you, to ensure you are on the right path to living a successful life as an adult. Share if there is something specific you need their assistance with.
- Thank God for all the advocates in your life that are praying for you and helping you.

DAY 5: PUSH THROUGH

- Try to recite this week's verse out loud without looking.
- The Holy Spirit inspired the disciples to remember what

they experienced with Jesus, which allowed some of them to write the books in the Bible. How do you plan to tell others about God and what He's done in your life?

❑ Recite this week's scripture again.

❑ Pray that the Holy Spirit helps you share with others what you've learned about Jesus, so others will also come to know the good news of the Gospel.

DAY 6: PRACTICE MAKES PERFECT

❑ Try again to recite this week's verse out loud. Spend time practicing until you can almost say it from memory.

❑ Your coach or parent advocates for you by recommending changes that can make you better both on and off the field. Do you follow their suggestions? The Holy Spirit also speaks to your heart, prompting you to make changes in your thinking and behavior. Do you listen to His suggestions?

❑ Pray that God helps you to consider all the help you have from the advocates in your life.

DAY 7: FINISH STRONG

❑ Recite this week's verse. Spend time practicing until you can say it from memory.

❑ As you read through this devotion and your Bible, the Holy Spirit is helping you remember what you've read and will also help you recall the information later in life during moments when you need it. How will this help when you face difficult situations in the future?

❑ Thank God for the gift of the Holy Spirit and all the help He is providing in your life.

❑ Close out this week by saying the scripture from memory.

I'VE GOT THE POWER

You will receive power when the Holy Spirit comes upon you. (Acts 1:8 NLT)

Superheroes are not regular humans. They have special abilities that allow them to defeat people and situations that the average person cannot. They may have **supernatural** strength, be able to fly, can see through walls, or some other ability that makes them very different from normal people.

When Jesus was **baptized**, the Holy Spirit came from heaven and settled on Him. Jesus received power at that moment, which allowed Him to heal the sick, raise the dead, cast out demons, and resist Satan's tricks. The Holy Spirit immediately comes to live inside of us when we ask Jesus to be our Savior, and we receive the same power.

WORD FOCUS:

supernatural — above or beyond what is natural

baptize — a religious ceremony where one goes underwater to express their faith

You've never seen a superhero with the ability to fly just running away from a bad guy, or one with superhuman strength balled up in a corner while getting beat up. But that's what we look like when we struggle with issues in life instead of using the power inside of us from the Holy Spirit to fight back. That power gives us the ability to defeat our enemy, to pray for others to be healed, and to live a life that makes God proud of us.

WEEK 15

You will receive power when the Holy Spirit comes upon you. (Acts 1:8 NLT)

DAY 1: WARM UP

- ❏ Read this week's verse out loud.
- ❏ How do you respond to negative things happening in your life? Do you have to accept whatever comes your way, or is there something you can do about it?
- ❏ Read the scripture out loud again.
- ❏ Pray for God to speak to you this week about the power inside of you from the Holy Spirit.

DAY 2: BREAK IT DOWN

- ❏ Read this week's verse out loud.
- ❏ Rewrite the scripture in your own words and make it personally about you.
- ❏ Do you feel like you need power in your life right now? What specifically do you need it for?

❑ Pray that God helps you understand how to use the power He has given you through the Holy Spirit.

DAY 3: GET IN POSITION

❑ Read this week's verse out loud.
❑ God has a special purpose for each of our lives, but to accomplish it, we must follow the Holy Spirit's direction, and work through His power to be successful. Is there something you think you are supposed to do in your life that you need help from the Holy Spirit on?
❑ Repeat the scripture out loud.
❑ Ask the Holy Spirit to help you accomplish what God wants you to do with your life.

DAY 4: HUDDLE UP

❑ Read this week's verse out loud.
❑ Discuss with your parent, coach, or other trusted adult why you think Jesus didn't perform miracles until the Holy Spirit came on Him. Discuss all the things Jesus was able to do by the power of the Holy Spirit.
❑ Pray together that you will experience the power of the Holy Spirit in the same way Jesus did.

DAY 5: PUSH THROUGH

❑ Try to recite this week's verse out loud without looking.
❑ One form of power from the Holy Spirit is the ability to have characteristics you may not normally have, like courage, boldness, and wisdom. How can these qualities benefit you

and others around you?

❑ Recite this week's scripture again.

❑ End today's workout by praying for the Holy Spirit to bring out the positive qualities you desire in your life but don't currently have.

DAY 6: PRACTICE MAKES PERFECT

❑ Try again to recite this week's verse out loud. Spend time practicing until you can almost say it from memory.

❑ The Holy Spirit is supposed to be a constant presence in your life so He can support you in your Christian walk. Are you aware of His presence and seeking His power when you need help?

❑ Pray that you would always be aware of the Holy Spirit's support that is available to help you.

DAY 7: FINISH STRONG

❑ Recite this week's verse. Spend time practicing until you can say it from memory.

❑ Having the Holy Spirit in your life is like having a star player on your team that dominates the competition. How can the Holy Spirit's power give you an advantage when you are facing difficult times?

❑ Thank God for the power of the Holy Spirit available in your life and pray you will not let it sit inside of you unused.

❑ Close out this week by saying the scripture from memory.

Section 4:

WHO AM I?

CUSTOM MADE

I will praise You, for I am fearfully and wonderfully made. (Psalms 139:14 NKJV)

When you look in the mirror, do you like the image staring back at you? People may wish they were taller or had different hair and a smaller nose. Some athletes wish they could run faster, hit harder, or throw further. Sometimes it can be tough to accept yourself the way you were born.

When we look at our image, we must remember that God **uniquely** created us. In a world with billions of people, there is absolutely no one else like us. Being fearfully made means that God showed great respect and honor when He formed us. He took His time to make sure we were created exactly how He wanted so we would be wonderfully made.

When we want to change certain things about ourselves or don't like our physical features, we are rejecting part of God's creation and His gift to us. God made a world full of beautiful places, things, and people, and you are a part of His wonderful creation. Praise God for the fearful and wonderful way He created you.

> **WORD FOCUS:**
>
> **unique** – different, unlike something else

WEEK 16

I will praise You, for I am fearfully and wonderfully made. (Psalms 139:14 NKJV)

DAY 1: WARM UP

❑ Read this week's verse out loud.

❑ How do you feel about the way God created you? Are you feeling thankful, dissatisfied, or somewhere in-between about the way God made you?

❑ Read the scripture out loud again.

❑ Pray that God will reveal how you are fearfully and wonderfully made.

DAY 2: BREAK IT DOWN

❑ Read this week's verse out loud.

❑ Rewrite the scripture in your own words and make it personally about you.

❑ Some people believe they are accidents and wonder why they are even on earth. What does this scripture tell you about that belief?

❑ Thank God for specifically making you exactly the way you are.

DAY 3: GET IN POSITION

- ❏ Read this week's verse out loud.
- ❏ God intentionally created you just the way you are. What do you think He would say if you asked Him to look differently? How do you think God feels when we wish we could change how He made us?
- ❏ Repeat the scripture out loud.
- ❏ Pray that you would understand you are made exactly the way God wanted you to be.

DAY 4: HUDDLE UP

- ❏ Read this week's verse out loud.
- ❏ Talk to your parent, coach, or other trusted adult about how you feel about yourself. Are there any areas about yourself you're struggling with accepting? Discuss and share your specific concerns.
- ❏ Pray together that you would realize you were created exactly how you were supposed to look, with the skills and talents God wanted you to have.

DAY 5: PUSH THROUGH

- ❏ Try to recite this week's verse out loud without looking.
- ❏ Do you remember making art projects and gifts for your parents when you were younger? How did they respond? Did they ever want to change something about it? How does this relate to this week's scripture?
- ❏ Recite this week's scripture again.

❑ Pray that you would understand how much you are loved, and how much thought went into creating you.

DAY 6: PRACTICE MAKES PERFECT

❑ Try again to recite this week's verse out loud. Spend time practicing until you can almost say it from memory.

❑ If you always compared yourself to others, you'd probably be able to find something about other people you wish you had, like a physical feature or a talent. God made everything about you with passion. Can you accept you were created exactly how you were supposed to be?

❑ Pray that you would accept all of the unique characteristics God purposefully created in you.

DAY 7: FINISH STRONG

❑ Recite this week's verse. Spend time practicing until you can say it from memory.

❑ Earlier, you learned God was the Potter who specifically created you. This week, you learned you were created with great feeling by God. How does it make you feel to know you were so passionately created? What can you do from today on to show God how much you appreciate the way He created you?

❑ Thank God for doing such a wonderful job when He created you and ask that He would help you always accept yourself.

❑ Close out this week by saying the scripture from memory.

THE STORY OF YOU

You saw me before I was born. Every day of my life was recorded in your book. Every moment was laid out before a single day had passed. (Psalms 139:16 NLT)

Before an author writes a book, they must first form the story details in their mind. They decide who the main character will be, what they will look like, details about their personality, and anything else important for the story they want to tell. The author will form the character's words, thoughts, feelings, and actions that take place throughout the entire story.

You are the main character of your story. God carefully watched your development when you were still in your mother's belly, to make sure you formed according to His plan. He knew what your favorite color would be, your favorite food, and your favorite smell. He also knew what your personality would be like. And then He **documented** every day of your life.

God has specifically designed plans for you. He knows if you will go to college, whether you'll get married and if you'll have children. He knows what your career will be and what kind of impact

WORD FOCUS:

documented – to write, record, or capture a person or event you'll make on the world. Even when bad things happen, they are never a surprise to Him. There is no need to worry about your future because you can trust that God has written your story for His glory.

WEEK 17

You saw me before I was born. Every day of my life was recorded in your book. Every moment was laid out before a single day had passed. (Psalms 139:16 NLT)

DAY 1: WARM UP
- ❑ Read this week's verse out loud.
- ❑ The details of your entire life are already known by God. How does that make you feel, based on what you now know about God?
- ❑ Read the scripture out loud again.
- ❑ Pray that you will be able to trust God with His plan for your life.

DAY 2: BREAK IT DOWN
- ❑ Read this week's verse out loud.
- ❑ Rewrite the scripture in your own words and make it personally about you.
- ❑ This scripture is more proof that no one is an accident, but

that everyone's life was planned by God. Does this change anything you previously thought about yourself? How can you use this verse to encourage someone else who is not happy with their life?

❑ Pray that you will be able to share this scripture to encourage someone else about their life.

DAY 3: GET IN POSITION

❑ Read this week's verse out loud.

❑ God always knew everything you would do, as He planned your life out before you were born. He gave you a unique personality, which helps determine the choices you make. How do you think your personality has affected the direction of your life?

❑ Repeat the scripture out loud.

❑ Thank God for the unique way He created you.

DAY 4: HUDDLE UP

❑ Read this week's verse out loud.

❑ Discuss with your parent, coach, or other trusted adult what they think about having their entire life already known by God. Talk about how it makes each of you feel, and how it impacts the way you trust God.

❑ Share the verse you are learning today and ask if they have any further thoughts.

❑ Pray together, thanking God for the plan He has already created for your lives.

DAY 5: PUSH THROUGH

- ❏ Try to recite this week's verse out loud without looking.
- ❏ Do you like the way God made you? Do you wish your personality were different? Would you rather be more outgoing or funny? Are you naturally shy? Write down three things about your personality that you like and why, and then do the same thing for three traits you don't like.
- ❏ Recite this week's scripture again.
- ❏ Pray that God would help you accept those things you don't like about yourself and that He would show how they can help you complete the purpose He created you for.

DAY 6: PRACTICE MAKES PERFECT

- ❏ Try again to recite this week's verse out loud. Spend time practicing until you can almost say it from memory.
- ❏ God is what we call omniscient, which means He knows everything, even the details about all your family and friends, and even complete strangers. What does this mean for you and your future?
- ❏ Pray for others God has put in your life, that He would use you to help them, and use them to help you.

DAY 7: FINISH STRONG

- ❏ Recite this week's verse. Spend time practicing until you can say it from memory.
- ❏ We learned that God is the all-knowing author of your life. From the beginning, He has written an amazing story about

you, and it is full of His love and care. Finish this week writing a statement about how you will trust God with the story of your life.

- ❑ Thank God for writing your story, and pray that you will always trust Him, even when there are times that you don't like your story.
- ❑ Close out this week by saying the scripture from memory.

HANDCRAFTED

For we are God's handiwork, created in Christ Jesus to do good works, which God prepared in advance for us to do.

(Ephesians 2:10 NIV)

Craft shows allow people to display their creative ability to make beautiful things with their hands. Every item starts in the imagination of the person who created it. After a picture or idea is formed in their mind, the artist then uses their hands to create it. No one item is exactly like another, even when they are made by the same person.

You were **handcrafted** by God into the work of art that you see in the mirror. When God created you, He had a special purpose in mind, and there are things He planned for you to accomplish, and He designed you with what you need to complete those tasks. Once we accept Jesus into our lives, we are then *in Christ*, and we start living through His power, which helps us to make good choices and do good things.

> **WORD FOCUS:**
>
> **handcrafted** – made by hand

Remember that you are uniquely designed by God's hands. There are things He has planned for you, that no one else in this world can do. When you're feeling jealous of someone else's life, talents, or athletic abilities, remember that if you were like them, you wouldn't be able to accomplish those specific tasks for God that *only you* can complete.

WEEK 18

For we are God's handiwork, created in Christ Jesus to do good
works, which God prepared in advance for us to do.
(Ephesians 2:10 NIV)

DAY 1: WARM UP

❑ Read this week's verse out loud.

❑ Why do you think you were created? Did you know you were created to do good works? What good have you done so far?

❑ Read the scripture out loud again.

❑ Pray that God would help you better understand what good you were created to do.

DAY 2: BREAK IT DOWN

❑ Read this week's verse out loud.

❑ Rewrite the scripture in your own words and make it personally about you.

❑ Because Jesus died on the cross for your sins, you can do many good works through Him. How do you think Jesus helps you to do good things?

❏ Thank Jesus for His power working inside of you that helps you do good works.

DAY 3: GET IN POSITION

❏ Read this week's verse out loud.

❏ There may be disappointing and painful experiences you may have gone through or will experience in the future. Other people may experience similar situations you could help with. Discuss ways that a bad experience can turn into something good.

❏ Pray that God will help you use difficult times in your life to help others.

DAY 4: HUDDLE UP

❏ Read this week's verse out loud.

❏ Knowing that God has already created and prepared good works for you to do, discuss with your parent, coach, or other trusted adult how your actions won't just affect you—they will also have an impact on your family, friends, teammates, community, and even society at large as you grow older. How great of an impact do you think you can make?

❏ Share the verse you are learning today and ask if they have any additional thoughts.

❏ Pray together that you would be brave enough to do big things for God.

DAY 5: PUSH THROUGH

❑ Try to recite this week's verse out loud without looking.

❑ As you learned last week, your entire life has been laid out by God, which He recorded. He knew the exact point when you would receive Jesus Christ in your life, and from that moment on, He designed a plan of good works that only you can do. How can this help you from being jealous about what other people are doing?

❑ Recite this week's scripture again.

❑ End by praying that God will help you stay focused on the good you are supposed to do, and not be jealous about what other people are doing.

DAY 6: PRACTICE MAKES PERFECT

❑ Try again to recite this week's verse out loud. Spend time practicing until you can almost say it from memory.

❑ There are over 7.5 billion people on the earth. Out of all those people, God created you to complete tasks no one else can do like you do. There are people that only you can reach. How important do you think you are, knowing this information?

❑ Pray that God will give you the confidence to do good works for the people He has put in your life.

DAY 7: FINISH STRONG

❑ Recite this week's verse. Spend time practicing until you can say it from memory.

❏ God formed you in His mind before He created you with His hands. Close out this week reminding yourself you are significant and were created for a specific reason and purpose, and there's work that God has planned and prepared for you to do. How will everything you are learning help you accomplish what God created you to do?

❏ Pray that God helps you remember and use all the knowledge you've learned each time you are supposed to do the good works He's planned for you.

❏ Close out this week by saying the scripture from memory.

CONFIDENCE FOR YOUR TOMORROW

For I know the plans I have for you, declares the LORD, plans to prosper you and not to harm you, plans to give you a hope and a future. (Jeremiah 29:11 NIV)

Sometimes we experience difficult situations in life that seem unfair. Your parents may be getting a divorce and breaking up your family while your friend seems to have a perfect life at home. You may have gotten injured again and are out for the season while your teammate continues to stand out on the field. You might be struggling in that one subject while your classmate gets straight As with little effort.

Because we are not on the same level as God, we can't begin to understand why difficult things happen in our lives. But you have learned that God has a specific plan just for you, and He knows how everything in your life is going to work out. This doesn't mean His plan will always feel good, but you must understand it is not meant to hurt you, but rather to **prosper** you and give you a bright future.

WORD FOCUS:

prosper – to grow or succeed

There may be times when you wish your life were different, but remember everything you are experiencing is a part of God's amazing plan. Even though it may not feel like it right now, God is going to use every tough experience, every tear, and every disappointment in His plans for your future.

WEEK 19

For I know the plans I have for you, declares the LORD, plans to prosper you and not to harm you, plans to give you a hope and a future. (Jeremiah 29:11 NIV)

DAY 1: WARM UP

- ❏ Read this week's verse out loud.
- ❏ This week we read more about the plans God has for you, which provides more information about your future. What kind of hope do you have for your future right now?
- ❏ Read the scripture out loud again.
- ❏ Pray that you will continue to learn about and understand the plans God has for you.

DAY 2: BREAK IT DOWN

- ❏ Read this week's verse out loud.
- ❏ Rewrite the scripture in your own words and make it personally about you.
- ❏ To prosper means to grow and improve. In what areas are you prospering right now (grades, sports, music, dance,

writing, etc.)? What do you need to continue to improve?

❑ Pray about the areas you feel you are not prospering in and ask God for His help.

DAY 3: GET IN POSITION

❑ Read this week's verse out loud.

❑ God has a master plan with your name on it, which affects your life. What kind of things do you worry about for your future? When you remember that God has a plan, how does that affect your worries?

❑ Repeat the scripture out loud.

❑ Ask God to help you give the worries you have about your future over to Him, and trust in the plan He has for your life.

DAY 4: HUDDLE UP

❑ Read this week's verse out loud.

❑ Have you ever asked, "Why me?" when something bad happened to you? Discuss with your parent, coach, or other trusted adult how unfortunate events don't change God's plans for your lives. In what ways can you encourage yourself when facing difficult times?

❑ Pray together that when bad things happen in life, you won't lose hope about your future.

DAY 5: PUSH THROUGH

❑ Try to recite this week's verse out loud without looking.

❑ Even when bad things happen, God still plans to accomplish good things in our lives. Can you trust God with your future, even when things aren't going well in your present?

❑ Recite this week's scripture again.

❑ Pray that you don't lose hope when experiencing difficult times by remembering they don't change God's plan for your future.

DAY 6: PRACTICE MAKES PERFECT

❑ Try again to recite this week's verse out loud. Spend time practicing until you can almost say it from memory.

❑ This week, you are once again reminded you are not an accident and that God has plans for you. Are you confident that you can still trust God when things don't seem to be going well in your life?

❑ Pray that God will remind you of the hope and future He has for you, especially when things get difficult in your life.

DAY 7: FINISH STRONG

❑ Recite this week's verse. Spend time practicing until you can say it from memory.

❑ We close out this week knowing that God has a plan to improve us and not hurt us, so He can give us hope for our future. Living in a sinful world, you will face difficult experiences. How does this week's scripture change your thoughts about your future?

❑ Thank God for His plans for you and pray that you never lose hope about your future.

❑ Close out this week by saying the scripture from memory.

A GUARANTEED WIN

Yet in all these things we are more than conquerors through Him
who loved us. (Romans 8:37 NKJV)

Have you ever heard of a game being fixed? Fixing a contest means deciding who will win before the competition starts. This is a situation where the players, coaches, or referees know ahead of time what team should win, and they may do certain things during the competition to dishonestly affect the outcome. There is only one situation where fixing a fight is completely acceptable—and that's when it's your life.

You have tasks assigned for you to **accomplish**. But you also have an opponent who is determined to completely destroy all those plans that God has for your life. Your life is fixed because no matter how much your opponent tries to defeat you, you will always come out as the champion. Jesus won every victory for you when He died on the cross.

Each situation you'll face for the rest of your life has been fixed. No matter what you are up against and no matter what problems come your way, you will win! It doesn't matter if the struggle is happening

> **WORD FOCUS:**
>
> **accomplish** — to achieve or complete something

right now, next week, or years from now. When Jesus is involved, it will always be a fixed fight that you will win.

WEEK 20

Yet in all these things we are more than conquerors through Him who loved us. (Romans 8:37 NKJV)

DAY 1: WARM UP

❑ Read this week's verse out loud.

❑ How would you feel if you knew you would always win any game, contest, or competition you entered? How would that affect your confidence?

❑ Read the scripture out loud again.

❑ Pray that God would show you that you are always a winner through Jesus.

DAY 2: BREAK IT DOWN

❑ Read this week's verse out loud.

❑ Rewrite the scripture in your own words and make it personally about you.

❑ To conquer means to win or overcome someone or something. Your life has been carefully planned out with great detail by someone bigger and stronger than anything. Is there a challenging situation you need His help with?

- ❏ Pray that you will always remember God is greater than anything you'll ever face.

DAY 3: GET IN POSITION
- ❏ Read this week's verse out loud.
- ❏ Winning in life doesn't always mean things will turn out the way you want them to. But it does mean God will use the outcome of every situation you face in His plan for your life. Can you think of a situation where something didn't go as planned, but still worked out in the end? What did you learn from that experience?
- ❏ Repeat the scripture out loud.
- ❏ Pray that God helps you trust Him even when things don't turn out the way you planned.

DAY 4: HUDDLE UP
- ❏ Read this week's verse out loud.
- ❏ Discuss with your parent, coach, or other trusted adult about what winning means to them. How important is winning athletic events? What about card or board games? Contests? How is this different than this week's theme?
- ❏ Pray together that you understand when winning is and is not important.

DAY 5: PUSH THROUGH
- ❏ Try to recite this week's verse out loud without looking.
- ❏ Being a conqueror has nothing to do with our ability. It is only because God loves us so much. Do you think you

deserve this special treatment? Why or why not?

❑ Recite this week's scripture again.

❑ End by thanking God for loving you so much and blessing you to be a conqueror.

DAY 6: PRACTICE MAKES PERFECT

❑ Try again to recite this week's verse out loud. Spend time practicing until you can almost say it from memory.

❑ During a competition, it may look like the other side is winning. But when you are a conqueror, you will eventually overcome your opponent. Is there a situation that doesn't seem to be going your way? Do you believe that things can change?

❑ Pray that you never lose hope that God will always allow you to be a conqueror, no matter how bad things may look.

DAY 7: FINISH STRONG

❑ Recite this week's verse. Spend time practicing until you can say it from memory.

❑ As you close out this week and section, remember who you are and that God has made you a conqueror, and He has planned every situation you'll ever experience. How will this information help you trust God when you are facing difficult times?

❑ Thank God for all the ways He is helping you to win in life.

❑ Close out this week by saying the scripture from memory.

Section 5:

WHO IS MY OPPONENT?

THE BIGGEST LOSER

I saw Satan fall like lightning from heaven. (Luke 10:18 NKJV)

There was once a beautiful angel in heaven named Lucifer, whose name meant 'bringing light'. The Bible reveals a **flawless** description of Lucifer, as he was full of wisdom and beauty, and was covered by every precious gemstone, which were all set in gold. He was the highest of angels, but unfortunately, that powerful position became too much for Lucifer to handle.

Pride grew in his heart, and he wanted all the glory and power that belonged to God. In his evil desire to become like God, he convinced one-third of the angels in heaven to join him in an epic battle to take over God's throne. By the time it was over, Lucifer and his army were kicked out of heaven, and his name was changed to Satan, which means "adversary" or *enemy*.

WORD FOCUS:

flawless – perfect, without fault or defect

Satan has been trying to defeat God ever since, but God is too great and powerful, and Satan is no match for Him. Since God created and loves us, Satan tries to get back at Him by hurting us. We are now Satan's enemies also, and he is constantly planning ways to harm us. The best way to defeat an enemy or opponent is to learn about them, so we can be prepared and know how to beat them.

WEEK 21

I saw Satan fall like lightning from heaven. (Luke 10:18 NKJV)

DAY 1: WARM UP

❑   Read this week's verse out loud.

❑   When you hear the word Satan or devil, what comes to mind? Before today's devotion, what did you know about Satan?

❑   Read the scripture out loud again.

❑   Pray for God to help you learn more about your enemy so you can defeat him.

DAY 2: BREAK IT DOWN

❑   Read this week's verse out loud.

❑   In Ezekiel 28, we find a description of Satan that includes him being described as a "model of perfection, full of wisdom, and perfect in beauty." Why do you think someone that had so many amazing qualities would turn bad?

❑   Finish your workout thanking God for all the qualities and talents He's given you and ask Him to help you never take them for granted or become prideful.

DAY 3: GET IN POSITION

❑ Read this week's verse out loud.

❑ Satan's original name was Lucifer, which we learned means bringing light. We usually associate light with knowledge and truth. Since he was kicked out of heaven and his name was changed, Satan is now associated with evil, darkness, and lies. How do you think Satan uses all the knowledge and truth he has against us?

❑ Repeat the scripture out loud.

❑ Ask God for wisdom and knowledge so you will not be tricked by Satan.

DAY 4: HUDDLE UP

❑ Read this week's verse out loud.

❑ Satan is described as covered in every precious stone, including a diamond, ruby, emerald, and sapphire, all set in gold, and created just for him. Discuss with your parent, coach, or other trusted adult how all those priceless things weren't enough for Satan, as he still wanted more power. What lesson can you learn from this?

❑ Pray together that you would always be grateful and appreciate the gifts that God has given you.

DAY 5: PUSH THROUGH

❑ Try to recite this week's verse out loud without looking.

❑ Satan was in the Garden of Eden and started his plan to get back at God by deceiving Eve and bringing sin to the humans God created. He also tried to deceive Jesus but was unsuccessful. Why do you think Satan succeeded against Eve but was unsuccessful against Jesus?

❑ Recite this week's scripture again.

❑ End by praying that God will help you be aware of Satan's tricks directed toward you and that you'll know how to respond.

DAY 6: PRACTICE MAKES PERFECT

❑ Try again to recite this week's verse out loud. Spend time practicing until you can almost say it from memory.

❑ One of the best ways to beat an opponent is by learning from someone who has previously defeated him. Satan was thrown out of heaven after he tried to take God's position, and we know that He could not defeat Jesus. What have you learned so far in this devotional that can help you defeat Satan as well?

❑ Pray that God shows you what you need to do to beat Satan when he targets you.

DAY 7: FINISH STRONG

❑ Recite this week's verse from memory.

❑ This week, we learned how a perfectly created angel let pride take over and ruin his life. Now, Satan wants to ruin our lives as well. But no matter what his plan is against us, we know he's been defeated before, so we can defeat him again. Takes notes as you go through this section, to be aware of the strategies he will try to use against you.

❑ Pray that God will open your eyes to all the ways Satan will try to beat you so you will be ready to respond.

❑ Close out this week by saying the scripture from memory.

CRIMINAL ACTIVITY

The thief's purpose is to steal and kill and destroy.

(John 10:10 NLT)

A good coach will watch the competition and form a strategy to win based on the weaknesses they see on the other team and the strengths of their own team. In life, you have an opponent you are trying to beat, but this isn't the kind of game that you're used to playing—it's much more serious.

Your opponent has three goals: to *steal* what God has given you, to *kill* your hopes and dreams and eventually your life, and to *destroy* the plan God has for you. He goes by different names—Satan, Beelzebub, the devil, prince of evil, and prince of darkness. Whatever name you use, one thing is clear— he is your enemy, and he will use every dirty trick he knows to try to accomplish his goals.

The Holy Spirit is like a coach we can go to for guidance to help us overcome this most dangerous competitor, as He knows all about him and how we can beat him. The Bible teaches us the strategies our enemy will try to use against us. We must know them so we can defeat him when he attacks. Our lives and our future depend on it.

WEEK 22

The thief's purpose is to steal and kill and destroy.

(John 10:10 NLT)

DAY 1: WARM UP

- ❏ Read this week's verse out loud.
- ❏ How does it make you feel to know you have an enemy who wants to harm you? What do you think you should do about that?
- ❏ Read the scripture out loud again.
- ❏ Pray for God to show you how to stay safe from Satan's plans to hurt you.

DAY 2: BREAK IT DOWN

- ❏ Read this week's verse out loud.
- ❏ Rewrite the scripture in your own words and make it personally about you.
- ❏ This is a serious situation. Your opponent is not just trying to beat you, his goal is to completely destroy you, so it's very important that you are protected. Is there anything you have learned from your playbook that you think will help to keep you safe?
- ❏ Pray that you will understand how to use what you've learned about God, Jesus, and the Holy Spirit to defeat your

opponent.

DAY 3: GET IN POSITION

- ❏ Read this week's verse out loud.
- ❏ There are many tools Satan can use to accomplish his mission of stealing, killing, and destroying. He can use other people, popular things in culture, or even your desires. How can you be on guard to make sure he doesn't trick you with any of these?
- ❏ Repeat the scripture out loud.
- ❏ Ask God for help in identifying anything in your life Satan may be using to try and hurt you, and then ask for wisdom on how to respond.

DAY 4: HUDDLE UP

- ❏ Read this week's verse out loud.
- ❏ Even though you have an enemy making plans against you, you also have a team that can help you. Share this week's scripture with your parent, coach, or other trusted adult, and discuss the people in your life that can help and protect you from your enemy.
- ❏ Pray together that you will know who to contact when you need assistance and protection from evil plans.

DAY 5: PUSH THROUGH

- ❏ Try to recite this week's verse out loud without looking.
- ❏ One way to beat a competitor is to understand their plan of attack against you, and also any weaknesses they may

have. How can you learn more about Satan and how to beat him?

❑ Recite this week's scripture again.

❑ End by praying that you will learn more about your enemy so you can develop a plan for how to beat him.

DAY 6: PRACTICE MAKES PERFECT

❑ Try again to recite this week's verse out loud. Spend time practicing until you can almost say it from memory.

❑ Sometimes coaches will watch other competitors to learn about them, to create a plan to beat them. In addition to everything you've already learned about the Holy Spirit, He is also your spiritual coach. He'll show you what you need to do to beat your opponent, but you have to follow His directions. In what ways do you think the Holy Spirit can coach you to victory?

❑ Pray that you will be able to understand the Holy Spirit's direction as He coaches you against your opponent.

DAY 7: FINISH STRONG

❑ Recite this week's verse. Spend time practicing until you can say it from memory.

❑ Although God has a plan for your life, Satan wants to completely ruin that plan. As you continue to learn about your enemy's plan, take note of the different ways Satan will try to beat you. Why do you think it's important to learn this information about Satan?

❑ Pray that God will help you learn all the information you need to win against Satan when he tries to attack you.

❑ Close out this week by saying the scripture from memory.

THE ULTIMATE DECEIVER

He has always hated the truth, because there is no truth in him.
When he lies, it is consistent with his character; for he is a liar and
the father of lies. (John 8:44c NLT)

In the fairy tale *Little Red Riding Hood*, a young girl went to visit her sick grandmother. On her way, she meets a wolf who convinces her to stop and pick flowers, while he goes to her grandmother's house and eats her. He also eats Little Red Riding Hood after tricking her into thinking he was her sick grandmother. From the moment the wolf met Little Red Riding Hood, he planned to **deceive** her, and it had a terrible outcome.

Lies make us believe something that is not true, usually so that we do something we weren't originally planning to do.

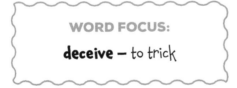

WORD FOCUS:

deceive – to trick

Satan is a master deceiver, and he wants to block every plan God has for us and keep us off the path He created for us to travel through in this life. Satan uses lies hoping to influence us to make choices he hopes will ruin the future God has planned for us.

It can be quite easy to fall for his tricks. Because he is the father of lies, every deception starts with Satan. We must never believe his lies and refuse to allow him to trick us into lying to others either. There is never a good reason to lie. Nothing good will ever happen when we choose to be dishonest.

WEEK 23

He has always hated the truth, because there is no truth in him. When he lies, it is consistent with his character; for he is a liar and the father of lies. (John 8:44c NLT)

DAY 1: WARM UP
- ❏ Read this week's verse out loud.
- ❏ Earlier in this devotional, we discussed the difference between the truth and a lie. How can knowing the difference affect the choices you make?
- ❏ Read the scripture out loud again.
- ❏ Pray for God to speak to you this week about the importance of rejecting lies in your life.

DAY 2: BREAK IT DOWN
- ❏ Read this week's verse out loud.
- ❏ Rewrite the scripture in your own words and make it personally about you.
- ❏ Since he is the father of lies, Satan created the concept of giving someone a false statement or idea with the hope

they will believe it. Why do you think people tell lies?

❑ Finish your workout by praying that God will help you determine when you have been given false information and keep you from being deceived.

DAY 3: GET IN POSITION

❑ Read this week's verse out loud.

❑ We learned a few weeks back about truth. When you get the urge to lie, you will also feel the Holy Spirit coach you to change your mind. Make sure you obey Him and ignore that popular sports apparel slogan—Just Don't Do It! When you want to tell a lie, how can you stop yourself at that moment?

❑ Repeat the scripture out loud.

❑ Pray that God would keep you from lying or spreading incorrect information, no matter how strong the urge to do so is.

DAY 4: HUDDLE UP

❑ Read this week's verse out loud.

❑ We must be careful not to deceive others, no matter how tempting. 'The Boy Who Cried Wolf' is a popular tale that warns against the dangers of lying. Discuss that story with your parent, coach, or other adult, and talk about how it relates to this scripture, and the price we must sometimes pay for our lies.

❑ Pray together that you will overcome any temptation to

lie, especially in an urgent situation, remembering that the truth is always best.

DAY 5: PUSH THROUGH

❑ Try to recite this week's verse out loud without looking.

❑ Deception is the ultimate weapon used to get someone to do what you want. It gives people incorrect information and understanding, with the purpose of faking the truth. This will usually cause them to respond in a way different from how they would if they knew the truth. Share a situation you responded to that was based on deception. How would you have responded differently if you knew the truth?

❑ Recite this week's scripture again.

❑ End by praying that your eyes would always be opened to learning and knowing the truth.

DAY 6: PRACTICE MAKES PERFECT

❑ Try again to recite this week's verse out loud. Spend time practicing until you can almost say it from memory.

❑ One thing we learned earlier about the Holy Spirit is that He will guide us into truth. When we pray and read our Bible, the Holy Spirit will help to open our eyes to the truth and help us overcome Satan's tricks, so that we don't fall for his dishonesty and deception. Are you spending time praying and reading your Bible so you can hear from the Holy Spirit? Are there any areas you can improve?

❑ Pray that you will be able to connect with the Holy Spirit so He can help you identify and reject lies and deception.

DAY 7: FINISH STRONG

❑ Recite this week's verse. Spend time practicing until you can say it from memory.

❑ We were first introduced to Satan in the Bible as the serpent. He deceived Eve into eating the fruit she was told not to eat by God, and as a result, she and Adam were kicked out of the beautiful Garden of Eden to suffer a hard life affected by sin. When we are deceived, the consequences can sometimes be awful, perhaps even worse than we could have ever expected. What can you do to always be aware of lies all around you?

❑ Pray that God would open your eyes and ears to identify situations when someone is trying to deceive you or lie to you.

❑ Close out this week by saying the scripture from memory.

ENEMY ON THE PROWL

Stay alert! Watch out for your great enemy, the devil. He prowls around like a roaring lion, looking for someone to devour. (1 Peter 5:8 NLT)

A lion is a skilled hunter. When they are on the **prowl**, they patiently study their surroundings for victims. They don't attack the strongest and fastest target. They will pounce on animals that aren't aware of their presence, so they don't get a head start on escaping. Lions also look for targets that are close by, weak or injured, and usually alone.

We are warned to be aware, as Satan stalks in the same way, looking to take us down. We must be on alert and aware of our emotions and thoughts.

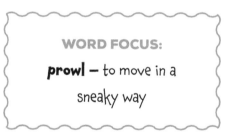

WORD FOCUS:

prowl – to move in a sneaky way

Sometimes, we may feel weak because we are angry or sad about something, and that can provide a perfect opportunity for the enemy to go after us.

To avoid his attack, it is also important for us to not be alone. We must have a strong group of friends and teammates to support and encourage us in difficult times. We need to build a strong circle that will encourage us to stay on the right track, not give in to temptation, and not give up. When you remain alert, you won't become easy prey, and the devil will look for someone else to attack.

WEEK 24

Stay alert! Watch out for your great enemy, the devil. He prowls around like a roaring lion, looking for someone to devour. (1 Peter 5:8 NLT)

DAY 1: WARM UP

- ❏ Read this week's verse out loud.
- ❏ How does it make you feel knowing you could be stalked by Satan at any time? What can you do to stay safe?
- ❏ Read the scripture out loud again.
- ❏ Pray for God to speak to you this week about how to stay safe from Satan as he looks for someone to attack.

DAY 2: BREAK IT DOWN

- ❏ Read this week's verse out loud.
- ❏ Rewrite the scripture in your own words and make it personally about you.
- ❏ Lions look for weak or injured victims to attack. You must know the Word of God, as Satan can easily influence someone who is weak and unsure of what to believe about

themselves or God. To resist His attacks, you must grow and stand strong in your faith.

❑ Finish your workout asking God to help you get stronger each day in your faith as you work through this devotional.

DAY 3: GET IN POSITION

❑ Read this week's verse out loud.

❑ If you find yourself far away from God and doing things you know you're not supposed to, you could be a target for Satan. Lions look for targets that are close by, so stay far from him by avoiding places you don't belong in, and don't hang with people who are bad influences and may encourage bad behavior. Are there people or actions you need to avoid in the future so you can move closer to God?

❑ Repeat the scripture out loud.

❑ Pray that you will be aware when you are moving away from God so you can make changes to move closer to Him.

DAY 4: HUDDLE UP

❑ Read this week's verse out loud.

❑ Strong groups are important when it comes to avoiding Satan's attacks. Share this week's scripture with your parent, coach, or other trusted adult and talk about the importance of strong relationships. There is safety in groups, so it's important to have people to talk to and grow with. Don't try to walk through life alone or think you don't need friends. How do you think your friends or teammates can help you avoid Satan's attacks?

❏ Pray together that you will form strong relationships that will keep you from being or feeling alone.

DAY 5: PUSH THROUGH

❏ Try to recite this week's verse out loud without looking.

❏ There is a key word in this week's scripture: like. As you work to avoid Satan's attacks, remember that he is not a lion, he only acts like one. Remember he is the father of lies, and this is just another lie he wants you to believe. Always remember that he wants to deceive you. How can the knowledge that Satan is acting like a lion help you to respond when you feel like you are being attacked?

❏ Recite this week's scripture again.

❏ End by praying that you will remember Satan is a deceiver and that you would be aware of his tricks when he is trying to attack you.

DAY 6: PRACTICE MAKES PERFECT

❏ Try again to recite this week's verse out loud. Spend time practicing until you can almost say it from memory.

❏ James 4:7 informs us that when we submit to God and resist the devil, he will flee or run away. You are resisting Satan by following the actions you have learned this week. What are some other ways you can resist Satan's attacks by submitting to God?

❏ Pray that God will show you different ways to submit to

Him as you resist attacks from Satan.

DAY 7: FINISH STRONG

❑ Recite this week's verse. Spend time practicing until you can say it from memory.

❑ As the father of lies, Satan is very good at making us believe something that is not true. This week we've learned more about how to resist his attacks—staying strong in our faith, forming good relationships, staying close to God, and knowing we can resist Satan's attacks because he is only acting like a lion and trying to deceive us. Which of these areas do you need to work on? How will you improve in that area?

❑ Pray that God will always help you as you grow stronger in your faith and continue to fight off Satan's attacks.

❑ Close out this week by saying the scripture from memory.

A BIG OLE TATTLETALE

For the accuser of our brothers and sisters has been thrown down to earth—the one who accuses them before our God day and night.
(Revelation 12:10b NLT)

A tattletale has one focus—to get you in trouble by reporting your bad behavior to someone in charge. Maybe it's your younger sibling who hits you first but runs and tells your parents if you hit them back. Or someone who encourages you to steal food from the cafeteria, and then reports you to the principal.

Satan is the **ultimate** tattletale. He tempts you to do stuff you know you shouldn't do, and as soon as you fall for his tricks, he runs back to God, pointing his finger at you. Maybe he thinks he can convince God not to love you anymore. Sometimes he accuses you in your own mind, hoping you will just give up.

WORD FOCUS:

ultimate – highest or best

When you are beating yourself up about something you know you shouldn't have done because a voice in your head won't let you forget it or forgive yourself, know that it is the voice of the accuser. He constantly looks for things to blame us for. Nothing Satan accuses us of matters because when Jesus died on the cross, He forgave us for it all.

For the accuser of our brothers and sisters has been thrown down
to earth—the one who accuses them before our God day and night.
(Revelation 12:10b NLT)

DAY 1: WARM UP
- ❑ Read this week's verse out loud.
- ❑ Do you know someone who is always telling on others?
  Why do you think they behave like that? When you feel like
  accusing someone else, how do you handle it?
- ❑ Read the scripture out loud again.
- ❑ Pray that God will show you a better way to respond when
  you want to accuse others.

DAY 2: BREAK IT DOWN
- ❑ Read this week's verse out loud.
- ❑ Rewrite the scripture in your own words and make it
  personally about you.
- ❑ When you do something wrong, Satan hopes to ruin your
  relationship with God by accusing you. But God sent His
  Son Jesus to die on the cross so that whatever you have
  been accused of can be forgiven. Is there anything in your

DAILY WORKOUT

life you need to forgive yourself for?

❑ Pray that God will help you forgive yourself and not believe Satan when he blames you.

DAY 3: GET IN POSITION

❑ Read this week's verse out loud.

❑ As the accuser, Satan also blames God for bad things that happen to us in life. He does this so we will get upset with God, and eventually turn our backs on Him due to disappointment and frustration. We must remember that God loves us and has a plan for our lives. Has Satan ever caused you to question if God is good, or if He even cares about you?

❑ Repeat the scripture out loud.

❑ Ask God to show you He can be trusted, no matter what you are going through.

DAY 4: HUDDLE UP

❑ Read this week's verse out loud.

❑ Satan wants to ruin the relationships with your family, friends, and teammates by highlighting their mistakes and accusing them every time they hurt you. Share this week's scripture with your parent, coach, or other trusted adult and discuss how you can respond to Satan's accusations when someone in your life offends you. What steps can you take to maintain your relationships, even if someone offends you?

- Pray together that God will keep your relationships healthy by helping you to work through conflict.

DAY 5: PUSH THROUGH

- Try to recite this week's verse out loud without looking.
- Because sin exists in the world, everyone makes mistakes. We must be ready to offer forgiveness to others, just like Jesus is always ready to forgive us. Just as we desire forgiveness for our mistakes, we must forgive others. Is there anyone you are having a hard time forgiving? Is there something someone needs to forgive you for?
- Recite this week's scripture again.
- End your workout by praying that God will allow you to give and receive forgiveness instead of blame.

DAY 6: PRACTICE MAKES PERFECT

- Try again to recite this week's verse out loud. Spend time practicing until you can almost say it from memory.
- When you live for God, you will always have an opponent who wants you to do and say things you know you shouldn't. Even though you may know his strategy to defeat you, there will be times when you don't respond the way you are supposed to, and he will use that against you. He doesn't want you to forgive yourself; he wants you to always feel guilty. Are there any mistakes you made for which you are having a hard time forgiving yourself?
- Pray that God will help you to forgive yourself of anything

you've done because He has already forgiven you.

DAY 7: FINISH STRONG

- ❏ Recite this week's verse. Spend time practicing until you can say it from memory.
- ❏ Accusing, blaming, or pointing fingers can all cause conflict in relationships. Satan wants to destroy your relationship with God and others and give you a negative view of yourself. Jesus' death on the cross allows us to be forgiven and for us to forgive others. How does it make you feel to know that there is nothing you can be accused of that God won't forgive? With His help, do you think you can forgive others, no matter what they do to hurt you? Is there something you feel like you cannot forgive?
- ❏ Pray that God will give you a heart that forgives others, as you accept forgiveness from Him.
- ❏ Close out this week by saying the scripture from memory.

Section 6:

WHAT SHOULD I DO?

CONFESSION TIME

But if we confess our sins, he is faithful and just to forgive us our sins and cleanse us from everything we've done wrong.

(1 John 1:9 CEB)

Every person that has ever walked this earth has sinned, except Jesus. Everyone has made bad choices in life—your mom, your dad, even your dear old grandmother. Remember, we were all born with the sinful nature that we will continue to struggle with for the rest of our lives. Every day we must decide whether we are going to make good choices or bad ones.

Jesus came to earth and gave up His life so He could **forgive** you for every bad choice you have made or will make. Nothing you can ever do is out of reach of His forgiveness; His death covered everything. All you have to do is admit to Him what you've done and ask for forgiveness, and He will remove it from your life.

WORD FOCUS:

forgive – to free from

When we say or do something we shouldn't, we must talk to Jesus about it. Sometimes we may feel too embarrassed, especially when it is something we have done repeatedly, even though we know it is wrong. There is nothing you can do that Jesus won't forgive, but you must confess it. No matter if it is a small offense, or something so awful you think you have ruined your life, Jesus is waiting for you to talk to Him about it.

WEEK 26

But if we confess our sins, he is faithful and just to forgive us our sins and cleanse us from everything we've done wrong.

(1 John 1:9 CEB)

DAY 1: WARM UP

❏ Read this week's verse out loud.

❏ As we've learned, there is nothing we can do to get rid of our sinful nature. Do you have temptations to do things you know you shouldn't, but sometimes may be hard to say no to? How do you handle those situations?

❏ Read the scripture out loud again.

❏ Pray for God to speak to you this week about the power of confession and forgiveness.

DAY 2: BREAK IT DOWN

❏ Read this week's verse out loud.

❏ Rewrite the scripture in your own words and make it personally about you.

❏ Is it hard for you to admit when you have done something

wrong? Do you have anything in your life you need to be forgiven of?

❏ Finish your workout by praying that Jesus will show you if there is anything in your life that still needs to be confessed to Him.

DAY 3: GET IN POSITION

❏ Read this week's verse out loud.

❏ We all make bad choices. We can be forgiven when we mess up, but we must be honest and admit to Jesus what we've done. He already knows, and there's nothing we can hide from Him, but He still wants us to come and talk to Him. Is it easy or difficult to talk to Jesus when you've made a mistake? Do you feel like He cares, or do you feel judged and ashamed?

❏ Repeat the scripture out loud.

❏ Decide to talk to Jesus about anything you've done that needs to be forgiven. Be honest as you confess what you've done and why.

DAY 4: HUDDLE UP

❏ Read this week's verse out loud.

❏ Sometimes our bad choices affect other people. After you've confessed to Jesus, determine if there is anyone else you need to talk to about what you've done. Share this week's scripture with your parent, coach, or other trusted adult and discuss how you should handle the discussion with that person. Write down your plan to confess and what you want to say.

❑ Pray together that you would have the courage to confess anything you've done that has impacted or hurt another person.

DAY 5: PUSH THROUGH

❑ Try to recite this week's verse out loud without looking.

❑ Once you've confessed your sins, Jesus is faithful to forgive, which means you don't have to wonder if He's forgiven you or not—He has! What does His forgiveness mean to you? How do you feel about being forgiven?

❑ Recite this week's scripture again.

❑ End by thanking Jesus for forgiving you of your sins and pray that you will always have the courage to come to Him when you make bad choices.

DAY 6: PRACTICE MAKES PERFECT

❑ Try again to recite this week's verse out loud. Spend time practicing until you can almost say it from memory.

❑ The final part of this scripture states that we will be cleansed from our unrighteousness. That means after Jesus forgives us, He no longer sees the bad things we confessed to Him, for we have been washed clean. We should no longer beat ourselves up or worry about what we've done. How does it feel knowing your sins are washed away forever?

❑ Thank Jesus for cleaning your life up and pray for His help in moving forward and not thinking about or dwelling on the past.

DAY 7: FINISH STRONG

❑ Recite this week's verse. Spend time practicing until you can say it from memory.

❑ As we wrap up this week, know that the "faithful and just" description of Jesus in this scripture guarantees that as long as you confess your sins, they will be forgiven, and they will be cleaned from your life. This doesn't mean you won't have to deal with consequences from a bad choice, but you won't have to walk around feeling guilty. Determine today not to carry the weight of bad choices in your life. How does it feel to be free from all the bad choices you have made after you ask for forgiveness?

❑ Pray that you will always have the courage to confess to Jesus when you need forgiveness and that you will accept forgiveness and release any shame, remembering that you have been washed clean.

❑ Close out this week by saying the scripture from memory.

TO HONOR AND OBEY

Children, obey your parents in the Lord, for this is right. "Honor your father and mother," which is the first commandment with promise: "that it may be well with you and you may live long on the earth." (Ephesians 6:1-3 NKJV)

There are different types of parents: biological, adoptive, step, or foster, to name a few. Whether your parents are kind and loving or mean and unsupportive, the Bible instructs you to **obey** and **honor** them.*

Obeying *in the Lord* means you shouldn't follow orders to do sinful or illegal things, harming others, or dishonoring God. The instruction to honor parents is a commandment with a promise attached to it. By honoring your parents, you are promised that things go well for you, and you will live a long life on earth.

Honoring parents is so important that God included it in the Ten Commandments, which are important rules in the Bible to follow. If you want to live well and live long, you should take care of yourself, eat healthy foods, make good choices, and

> **WORD FOCUS:**
>
> **obey** — to follow instructions or orders from another person
>
> **honor** — to show great respect

most importantly, honor your parents!

*__Please Note__ If you are experiencing abuse from your parents, please reach out to a coach, teacher, or other trusted adult for help.

WEEK 27

Children, obey your parents in the Lord, for this is right. "Honor your father and mother," which is the first commandment with promise: "that it may be well with you and you may live long on the earth." (Ephesians 6:1-3 NKJV)

DAY 1: WARM UP

- ❏ Read this week's verse out loud.
- ❏ God created parents to love, raise, and teach children as they grow into adults. Because of the sin in the world, every parent doesn't do this well, and sometimes other people must step in and help. How is your relationship with your parents? What would you like to improve in your relationship with them?
- ❏ Read the scripture out loud again.
- ❏ Pray for God to show you the importance of parents as you go through this week's workout.

DAY 2: BREAK IT DOWN

❏ Read this week's verse out loud.

❏ Rewrite the scripture in your own words and make it personally about you.

❏ Obeying parents can be hard, especially when they want you to do something that you don't want to do. But even if you don't want to, God commands you to obey your parents until you become an adult and move out on your own. Is it difficult for you to obey your parents? Share why you think obeying them can be hard.

❏ Finish your workout asking God to help you obey your parents, even when you don't feel like it.

DAY 3: GET IN POSITION

❏ Read this week's verse out loud.

❏ Honoring parents is something we must do throughout our entire lifetime, for as long as our parents are alive. No matter how old you are, you can always honor your parents by respecting them, speaking good about them, and never wishing harm on them, whether they deserve it or not. What are some specific ways you can honor your parents?

❏ Repeat the scripture out loud.

❏ End today's workout by praying that God would show you how to always honor your parents.

DAY 4: HUDDLE UP

❏ Read this week's verse out loud.

- Share this week's scripture with your parent, coach, or other trusted adult, and talk about the importance of honor and obedience. Discuss any concerns or struggles you may have with following this scripture and ask for specific advice. Write down ways you will try to obey and honor your parents this week.
- Pray together that you will follow through on your plan to obey and honor your parents.

DAY 5: PUSH THROUGH

- Try to recite this week's verse out loud without looking.
- Some children may have a hard time honoring their parents because of traumatic and painful experiences, but it is important that you still do the best you can to follow this scripture. Take time to think about any situation that may be negatively affecting your relationship with your parents. Is there anything you need to forgive your parents for?
- Recite this week's scripture again.
- End by praying that God would help you forgive your parents for any hurtful situations that make it hard for you to respect them.

DAY 6: PRACTICE MAKES PERFECT

- Try again to recite this week's verse out loud. Spend time practicing until you can almost say it from memory.
- When you obey and honor a parent, even when it's hard,

you show that you trust God enough to follow His way, even though you may not want to, or understand why you should. Obeying and honoring your parents gives you practice so you can also honor and obey God, which is one of the smartest things you could ever do. What are some ways you can honor and obey God?

❑ Pray that God will show you how to honor and obey Him.

DAY 7: FINISH STRONG

❑ Recite this week's verse. Spend time practicing until you can say it from memory.

❑ God gave you your parents for a reason. The Bible tells you how you should treat them, regardless of how your relationship is with them. If you wish you were born into a different family, remember that God does not make mistakes. What are some ways you can improve your relationship with your parents?

❑ Thank God for the parents He gave you and pray that He improves your relationship with them as you do your best to obey and honor them.

❑ Close out this week by saying the scripture from memory.

STAND OUT

And do not be conformed to this world, but be transformed by the renewing of your mind, that you may prove what is that good and acceptable and perfect will of God.

(Romans 12:2 NKJV)

As a young child, you picked up habits from **observing** others. You learned new words and believed things taught to you, not knowing if they were good or bad. There are many behaviors and beliefs that people learned growing up that don't agree with what the Bible teaches.

You don't have to look, sound, or behave like everyone else. Just because the popular group at school dresses a certain way doesn't mean you have to. Even if the best athlete on your team is taking harmful pills or drinks to perform better, that is not a reason for you to start. The influence of peer pressure is very strong, but you must keep your mind focused on making good choices that are pleasing to God.

WORD FOCUS:

observing — to watch

Don't be influenced by the wrong things or people. Companies pay famous people millions of dollars to influence you to buy their products. Your favorite athlete might support a shoe that won't help you perform better, or your favorite actress may promote food that isn't healthy for your body. When your mind is not affected by harmful things you see and hear, you can focus on living an acceptable life for God.

WEEK 28

And do not be conformed to this world, but be transformed by the renewing of your mind, that you may prove what is that good and acceptable and perfect will of God.

(Romans 12:2 NKJV)

DAY 1: WARM UP

❑ Read this week's verse out loud.

❑ Do you mind standing out or being different from everyone else? Or is it more important for you to fit in? Write down which describes you and why.

❑ Read the scripture out loud again.

❑ Pray for God to speak to you this week about how to determine His will for the way you should think, behave, dress, act, and speak.

DAY 2: BREAK IT DOWN

❑ Read this week's verse out loud.

- Rewrite the scripture in your own words and make it personally about you.
- Technology allows people to share their opinions about anything freely throughout the world, including new trends, words, and music. This can influence people positively or negatively. If enough people pick up on a new idea, it can soon become acceptable, even though it may not be positive. How do you know when new ideas are good or bad?
- Finish your workout by praying that God would help you identify good ideas from bad ones, no matter who or where they come from.

DAY 3: GET IN POSITION
- Read this week's verse out loud.
- To renew your mind means to refresh it from old ideas, thinking, or beliefs. When you renew your mind, you may come up with new ideas and new ways to do things. Your mind needs to be refreshed from all that the world has been feeding it, so you can identify how God desires for you to think, say, do, and act.
- Repeat the scripture out loud.
- Ask God for wisdom in identifying how He wants you to be different, instead of how the world wants you to be.

DAY 4: HUDDLE UP
- Read this week's verse out loud.

- ❑ Share this week's scripture with your parent, coach, or other trusted adult and discuss any pressure you may feel to be like others. Talk about the importance of standing for God and share ways you can stand out from everyone else.
- ❑ Pray together that God will give you the confidence to stand for Him, even if no one else will.

DAY 5: PUSH THROUGH

- ❑ Try to recite this week's verse out loud without looking.
- ❑ Do you ever want to buy certain products or dress a certain way because of someone else? Companies sometimes use famous people to sell products they have never used, to make other people want to buy them. There is always someone trying to influence you—whether at school, on your team, on TV, or social media. How can you be more aware of how others may be influencing your choices, and what should you do about it?
- ❑ Recite this week's scripture again.
- ❑ End by praying for God to help you be aware of all the areas that try to influence you, and that you would know how to respond.

DAY 6: PRACTICE MAKES PERFECT

- ❑ Try again to recite this week's verse out loud. Spend time practicing until you can almost say it from memory.
- ❑ When you renew your mind, it will lead to a transformation in your life. This means there will be major changes about

you that others will notice. God will notice as well, as He will be pleased with how you follow Him instead of others around you. This will help your life be pleasing and acceptable to Him. Are there any areas you already feel need changing?

❑ Pray that you will have the courage to transform areas of your life and that God will be pleased with those changes.

DAY 7: FINISH STRONG

❑ Recite this week's verse. Spend time practicing until you can say it from memory.

❑ Decide to renew your mind regularly, as sometimes our minds need a fresh restart, just like our electronics. You can refresh your mind by reading your Bible regularly, studying devotionals, attending church and youth groups, and talking with other friends who are Believers. Write down a plan for how you will renew your mind.

❑ Pray that God will help you transform your mind so that your life can be pleasing to Him.

❑ Close out this week by saying the scripture from memory.

SEARCH MISSION

And you will seek Me and find Me, when you search for Me with all your heart. (Jeremiah 29:13 NKJV)

In the movie, *God's Not Dead*, a young man who believed in God was challenged by his **Philosophy** professor to prove it. His entire grade depended on whether he could prove there was a God. The student then spent most of his first semester of college researching to provide evidence to his instructor and classmates that God was real. And he found it.

When God sees us asking questions, exploring our Bibles, and seeking to learn more about Him, He promises that we'll find what we are looking for. There are books, movies, science facts, and research that all tell us more about Him. God knows when we are really searching for more knowledge, and He will answer our questions.

God is available to us 24x7. We don't have to schedule an appointment or wait until He has finished

> **WORD FOCUS:**
>
> **philosophy** – the study of ideas and beliefs about knowledge and life

performing a miracle for someone else. He can use different ways to answer our questions about Him when we truly search for them. But we must seek with all of our heart.

WEEK 29

And you will seek Me and find Me, when you search for Me with all your heart. (Jeremiah 29:13 NKJV)

DAY 1: WARM UP

❑ Read this week's verse out loud.

❑ Every day you open this book, you are seeking more information about God. After everything you've read, how much do you feel you know about God? Are you clear or uncertain about what you've learned so far?

❑ Read the scripture out loud again.

❑ Pray for God to speak to you this week about ways you can seek to learn more about Him.

DAY 2: BREAK IT DOWN

❑ Read this week's verse out loud.

❑ Rewrite the scripture in your own words and make it personally about you.

❑ This week we learn that if we seek God, we will find out more about Him. Is there more information you would like to know about God?

❑ Finish your workout by praying that God will reveal himself to you more every time you seek Him.

DAY 3: GET IN POSITION

- ❏ Read this week's verse out loud.
- ❏ You may be reading some of the information in this book for the first time. As you have been working through each week, have you had a hard time believing something you've read? What can you do to get answers or find out more information?
- ❏ Repeat the scripture out loud.
- ❏ Ask God to show you where you can go to seek the specific information about Him that you are looking for.

DAY 4: HUDDLE UP

- ❏ Read this week's verse out loud.
- ❏ Share this week's scripture with your parent, coach, or other trusted adult and discuss if there are things about God they want more information on? Talk about ways you each can seek to learn more about Him. Agree to come back and share once you've found what you're looking for.
- ❏ Pray together that you would both find the answers you seek from God.

DAY 5: PUSH THROUGH

- ❏ Try to recite this week's verse out loud without looking.
- ❏ God created humankind so He could have a relationship with all of us. He wants to have your heart, so He can show all of himself to you. Is there any part of your heart or life you don't want God to see or know about?

- Recite this week's scripture again.
- End today's workout by praying that you would not hold anything about yourself from God.

DAY 6: PRACTICE MAKES PERFECT

- Try again to recite this week's verse out loud. Spend time practicing until you can almost say it from memory.
- As you seek God and build a relationship with Him, you will soon be able to hear His voice and know when He is talking directly to you about something. Have you ever heard God speak to you before? How did He speak to you, and how did you know it was Him?
- Pray that your relationship with God would grow stronger as you seek to learn more about Him.

DAY 7: FINISH STRONG

- Recite this week's verse. Spend time practicing until you can say it from memory.
- Think about the game of Hide and Seek you may have played as a child. God wants you to continue to seek Him until all your questions are answered. As you go through the rest of this book, God will be waiting for you to connect with Him, ask Him questions, and learn more about Him. How comfortable do you feel about seeking God and asking Him tough questions?
- Pray that you will always be confident to seek information from God and that you will continue to grow closer to Him.

❑   Close out this week by saying the scripture from memory.

EVIDENCE NOT NEEDED

We live by faith and not by sight. (2 Corinthians 5:7 CEB)

Faith is the *foundation* of Christianity. It takes faith to believe in a God you've never seen before. It takes faith to believe that Jesus rose from the dead when you didn't actually see it with your own eyes. It takes faith to believe He can live in your heart when it doesn't seem naturally possible. It takes faith to believe you'll go to heaven when you die when you have no idea where it is.

When you believe something, despite having no *evidence*, that's called faith. When you act on those beliefs, you are walking by faith. Most of what you've read in this book requires that you have faith to believe it. And once you believe it, the next step is to follow it. Walking by faith focuses on what you believe, instead of what you see.

> **WORD FOCUS:**
> **foundation** – base of support for something
> **evidence** – proof

People usually understand things by using the five senses, but faith can't be seen, smelled, tasted, felt, or heard. If we have no physical evidence of something, how do we know it's real?

This is the meaning of faith.

WEEK 30

We live by faith and not by sight. (2 Corinthians 5:7 CEB)

DAY 1: WARM UP

❑ Read this week's verse out loud.

❑ It takes little effort to use your senses while making a decision. Most of your decisions are based on what you see, hear, smell, taste, or feel. How do you usually make decisions when you don't have any evidence to support your choice?

❑ Read the scripture out loud again.

❑ Pray that God shows you how to walk by faith, and not always use your senses to make decisions.

DAY 2: BREAK IT DOWN

❑ Read this week's verse out loud.

❑ Rewrite the scripture in your own words and make it personally about you.

❑ To walk by faith, you believe and act on something without having physical proof to back it up. You can walk by faith by applying what you've learned from reading the Bible to your life. Can you think of a specific area in your life you can practice walking by faith in?

❑ Finish your workout by praying that God will show you areas in your life in which you can walk by faith.

DAY 3: GET IN POSITION

❑ Read this week's verse out loud.
❑ Walking by faith means you are going forward. It may start as a baby step, but apply the Word of God to your life with each next step. Are you stuck in a situation and are not sure how to proceed?
❑ Repeat the scripture out loud.
❑ Pray that God will give you direction for an area that you feel stuck in.

DAY 4: HUDDLE UP

❑ Read this week's verse out loud.
❑ Share this week's scripture with your parent, coach, or other trusted adult and ask them to discuss a situation that required them to walk by faith when they didn't know what the outcome would be. Discuss any feelings they may have had as they decided on how to move forward, and how they dealt with them.
❑ Pray together that you would have the confidence to walk by faith when you face a situation with an uncertain future.

DAY 5: PUSH THROUGH

❑ Try to recite this week's verse out loud without looking.
❑ Much of what you've read in this book each week requires faith to believe. You need faith to believe almost every

lesson in this book. Do you need evidence that what you've read is true before you follow the workouts, or have you been able to complete them by faith?

- ❏ Recite this week's scripture again.
- ❏ End today by praying that you will trust God and His Word, even when it may be hard to believe.

DAY 6: PRACTICE MAKES PERFECT

- ❏ Try again to recite this week's verse out loud. Spend time practicing until you can almost say it from memory.
- ❏ As you work through this book, your faith will continue to grow, and you will get more practice walking in faith, even when you don't know where it will lead you. How can walking by faith in smaller situations help you when facing bigger ones?
- ❏ Pray that God will build your strength every time you choose to walk by faith.

DAY 7: FINISH STRONG

- ❏ Recite this week's verse. Spend time practicing until you can say it from memory.
- ❏ As you grow older and learn more about God and the Bible, you will have more opportunities to walk by faith, which may impact not only your life, but the lives of others. Is there a specific area that you would like to impact the lives of others? Share an area you can walk by faith in now that will allow you to help other people.

❏ Pray that God would use your faith to touch the lives of others.

❏ Close out this week by saying the scripture from memory.

BLIND TRUST

Trust in the LORD with all your heart and lean not on your own understanding; in all your ways **submit** to him, and he will make your paths straight. (Proverbs 3:5-6 NIV)

Do you get nervous before a big game or a test? Many times, we may be anxious or nervous about something because we have already pictured a negative outcome in our minds. Do you spend a lot of time daydreaming about the future? Does it bring excitement or worry?

In life, the choices we make are usually based on our own understanding. Your understanding is what you believe will happen, but it is usually based on your knowledge and life experience. Your parents and coaches have many more years of life, so their understanding is probably greater than yours. But God has even more knowledge than them.

To trust in the Lord, we must have full confidence in His Plan. We show faith by trusting in God, instead of our feelings. When we trust in God instead

WORD FOCUS:

submit – surrender

of our thoughts, He will lead us on the correct way to go. Be brave enough to trust God each day with your life even when you don't know how everything is going to work out, because

He does.

WEEK 31

Trust in the LORD with all your heart and lean not on your own understanding; in all your ways submit to him, and he will make your paths straight. (Proverbs 3:5-6 NIV)

DAY 1: WARM UP

- ❏ Read this week's verse out loud.
- ❏ With everything going on in life, people can sometimes worry about how things will turn out. What kinds of situations in your life do you worry about?
- ❏ Read the scripture out loud again.
- ❏ Pray for God to show you what it means to trust Him with everything going on in your life.

DAY 2: BREAK IT DOWN

- ❏ Read this week's verse out loud.
- ❏ Rewrite the scripture in your own words and make it personally about you.
- ❏ Trusting in God requires that you be completely confident in Him, even though you don't know His plan for your life. Do you feel God can be trusted enough for you to stop

worrying about your life? Explain.

- ❏ Finish your workout by praying for enough confidence in God to always trust Him.

DAY 3: GET IN POSITION

- ❏ Read this week's verse out loud.
- ❏ The hardest thing about following this scripture is 'lean not on your own understanding', which means that sometimes you may have to ignore your feelings, no matter how strong they are, and how much you want to believe in them. What would it take for you to give up your own opinions or thoughts and trust in a different plan from God?
- ❏ Repeat the scripture out loud.
- ❏ Ask God for help in releasing your strong feelings and opinions to Him, so you can trust Him instead.

DAY 4: HUDDLE UP

- ❏ Read this week's verse out loud.
- ❏ Share this week's scripture with your parent, coach, or other trusted adult and discuss situations when they had to place their trust in God, even when they didn't know how things would turn out. Ask them to share how they felt while going through the experience.
- ❏ Pray together that you would learn how to trust God more than your own decisions.

DAY 5: PUSH THROUGH

- ❏ Try to recite this week's verse out loud without looking.

- The next step in this week's scripture is to submit all your ways to God. You can bring your decisions to God in prayer and see if He wants you to do something else instead, like not going to the school or team you wanted. Sometimes you must give up your decision and choose God's instead, as He knows both what you want and need. If you had to, could you give up your dream for God?
- Recite this week's scripture again.
- End by praying that you would be able to trust God with the future God has for you, even if is different from the future you planned for yourself.

DAY 6: PRACTICE MAKES PERFECT

- Try again to recite this week's verse out loud. Spend time practicing until you can almost say it from memory.
- When you submit your ways to God, the final part of this scripture shows that He will make your path straight. You don't have to be worried or anxious about your future or wonder what the right decision is when you have to make important choices. When you acknowledge God in everything you do, He will put you on the right path. Are there any choices about your future that you need direction for?
- Pray that you will remember to submit your ways to God so that He can direct the path for your future.

DAY 7: FINISH STRONG

- ❏ Recite this week's verse. Spend time practicing until you can say it from memory.
- ❏ God has given you the knowledge to make good decisions, but when that knowledge causes you to worry, that's when you must trust God instead of your own understanding of the situation and what you should do. What changes do you need to make in your life so you can follow these steps and trust God for your future?
- ❏ Thank God for showing you that as you trust and submit to Him, He will lead you on the right path to take.
- ❏ Close out this week by saying the scripture from memory.

TOSS IT OVER

Cast all your anxiety on him because he cares for you.

(1 Peter 5:7 NIV)

When my daughters were little and got upset about something that seemed big to them, I usually stepped in with a solution, wiping their tears and letting them know everything would be okay. As they've gotten older, sometimes they ask for my help, but most of the time they choose to handle things themselves. If they don't invite me to help, there's not much I can do, so they must figure things out on their own.

There are so many things in life out of our control that may cause us to be anxious. God cares about everything we are going through, everything that worries us, and everything we need help with. This week, we are taught to **cast** the things that worry us over to Him, so we need not be concerned about them anymore.

WORD FOCUS:

cast – to throw

When something is bothering us, we always have a choice—we can try to handle it ourselves, even though we may not know how to fix it, or we can hand it over to someone who knows exactly what to do. We were never meant to carry around the heavy weight that comes from holding on to anxious and fearful thoughts. God is there with outstretched hands, waiting for us to pass our concerns and worries over to Him.

WEEK 32

Cast all your anxiety on him because he cares for you.
(1 Peter 5:7 NIV)

DAY 1: WARM UP

❏ Read this week's verse out loud.
❏ How many things are you worried about today? Write them down, and how you have been dealing with them.
❏ Read the scripture out loud again.
❏ Pray for God to speak to you this week about handing over difficult situations to Him.

DAY 2: BREAK IT DOWN

❏ Read this week's verse out loud.
❏ Rewrite the scripture in your own words and make it personally about you.
❏ You are directed to cast difficult situations and thoughts over to God because He cares about you. This means He is really concerned about how you are doing and feeling every single day of your life. Write down who else in your life cares about you, and how they show it.

- [ ] Finish your workout thanking God for caring about you, and for all the people in your life that care about you as well.

DAY 3: GET IN POSITION

- [ ] Read this week's verse out loud.
- [ ] When you are dealing with worry or fear, it can cause you to make bad choices, get stuck in a position, and be unable to move forward. To live a productive life, you must get rid of things that are holding you back. What situations are you dealing with this week that are keeping you from moving forward?
- [ ] Repeat the scripture out loud.
- [ ] Pray that God will show you the situations in your life that you need to hand over to Him.

DAY 4: HUDDLE UP

- [ ] Read this week's verse out loud.
- [ ] Discuss with your parent, coach, or other trusted adult about things that may be giving you a lot of pressure – school grades, making the team, friendships, health issues, or problems at home. Share the situation and how it's been making you feel. Determine how you can cast them to God and stop worrying about them.
- [ ] Pray together that you will trust God with your situations and leave it in His hands to fix.

DAY 5: PUSH THROUGH

❑ Try to recite this week's verse out loud without looking.

❑ Next week, we'll discuss what to do after you've cast everything over to God. But today, it is important to remember that, after you've cast something to God, you don't take it back from Him. Many times, we give things over to God and things start to improve, then we take them back and mess them up again. Write down how you will leave situations in God's hands after you've given them to Him.

❑ Recite this week's scripture again.

❑ Pray that you will trust God enough to leave your situations in His hands and not take them back.

DAY 6: PRACTICE MAKES PERFECT

❑ Try again to recite this week's verse out loud. Spend time practicing until you can almost say it from memory.

❑ Review the list you made on Day 1. Many things can cause you to be anxious. Sometimes when you have multiple things going on in your life all at once, it can feel hopeless. It's important to cast things to God as quickly as possible so you're not dealing with multiple issues simultaneously. How will you know when something has reached a point when you need to give it to God? What signs will you look for?

❑ Pray that God will show you when you need to release situations to Him, so they don't affect you negatively.

DAY 7: FINISH STRONG

❑ Recite this week's verse. Spend time practicing until you can say it from memory.

❑ God cares for you and doesn't want you to deal with all the negative emotions worrying and fear brings. Tough situations can affect our physical and mental health, relationships, performance, and grades, so you must work to free yourself from anything negative that is affecting you. Write down a process you can follow to cast things over to God going forward, and steps you will take to leave them with Him.

❑ Pray that God will help you follow the plan you created to always cast your cares on Him.

❑ Close out this week by saying the scripture from memory.

PRAY, ASK, THANK

Do not be anxious about anything, but in every situation, by prayer and **petition**, with thanksgiving, present your requests to God. (Philippians 4:6 NIV)

Life sometimes doesn't go the way we want it to. There will always be something to worry about, whether it's school, sports, family problems, or peer pressure. When we worry or feel anxiety, it can often be distracting and cause us to do or act differently than we normally would. It can be hard to stop those feelings from coming when we experience difficult situations.

We have a step-by-step guide on what to do when we start to worry. As soon as we feel ourselves growing anxious, we must stop and pray about the situation. That means simply telling God what and how you are feeling in that moment. Next, ask Him for the help you need and let God know what you would like Him to do with the situation. Finally, as you pray, give thanks to God.

> **WORD FOCUS:**
>
> **petition** – to ask for something

After you have followed these steps, understand that you've done your part, and you have to trust God and wait for Him to respond. Don't forget that He knows all about you and can see the big plan He has for your life. When you feel yourself getting anxious again, repeat these steps to calm yourself and always remember— God's got everything under control.

WEEK 33

Do not be anxious about anything, but in every situation, by prayer and petition, with thanksgiving, present your requests to God. (Philippians 4:6 NIV)

DAY 1: WARM UP

❏   Read this week's verse out loud.

❏   This week's scripture provides more instruction on what do to when you're feeling anxious. You will always have needs, concerns, desires, and situations that may cause worry and concern. But there is an action you can take to respond to them. How have you been responding to tough situations since you started reading this book?

❏   Read the scripture out loud again.

❏   Pray for God to speak to you this week about the steps to take when you are feeling anxious or worried.

DAY 2: BREAK IT DOWN

❏   Read this week's verse out loud.

❏   Rewrite the scripture in your own words and make it

personally about you.

❏ Since no one can see into the future, there are times you may worry about how things will turn out. Once you feel yourself getting nervous, stop what you are doing, cast your thoughts to God, and calm your mind. Then you can follow the steps from this week's scripture. What are some ways you can quiet your thoughts?

❏ Pray that you would learn how to turn your worries over to God so you can stop worrying.

DAY 3: GET IN POSITION

❏ Read this week's verse out loud.

❏ To stop your mind from worrying, you must change your focus, and you do that by praying. Take your mind off your situation and move those thoughts to God instead. Tell Him what's going on in your life, and how you feel about it. Trust Him enough to share your deepest feelings. Write down the situation you want to talk to God about.

❏ Repeat the scripture out loud.

❏ Close out today's workout by talking to God about what's going on in your life. Spend more time than usual in prayer if you need to and be completely honest with how you are feeling.

DAY 4: HUDDLE UP

❏ Read this week's verse out loud.

❏ Discuss this week's scripture with your parent, coach, or

other trusted adult. Ask how they handle it when they are worried about situations in life. Find out if they have ever followed these steps before, and how things worked out for them. Write down any ideas you would like to try.

❑ Pray together that you will remember to give your worries to God instead of trying to figure things out on your own, and that you would not be scared to reach out to an adult when needed.

DAY 5: PUSH THROUGH

❑ Try to recite this week's verse out loud without looking.

❑ To petition God means to ask Him for something, just like you would ask your parents if you wanted something. God really wants you to come and talk to Him when you are anxious, as He cares for you. Be completely honest and write down what you want Him to do for you.

❑ Recite this week's scripture again.

❑ Finish your workout by talking to God about what you wrote down today. Open your heart to Him and let Him know how you feel and what you want.

DAY 6: PRACTICE MAKES PERFECT

❑ Try again to recite this week's verse out loud. Spend time practicing until you can almost say it from memory.

❑ The last step is to offer thanks to God while you are praying. Even though you don't know how He will answer your prayer, you can be thankful that He will do what's best for you. You can also give Him thanks for anything going on in your life. Make a list of what you are thankful for and use it to give thanks every time you pray.

❑ Spend time in prayer thanking God for the things and people you wrote on your list.

DAY 7: FINISH STRONG

❑ Recite this week's verse. Spend time practicing until you can say it from memory.

❑ Over the last two weeks, you've learned that God really cares about helping you when you're feeling worried about something, and He's given you steps to take to get His help. Write down the specific steps you will take every time you feel anxious, and bookmark this page so you can come back to it whenever you feel worried.

❑ Thank God for providing you with steps to take when you're feeling worried so that He can help you.

❑ Close out this week by saying the scripture from memory.

STRENGTH AND COURAGE

Have I not commanded you? Be strong and courageous. Do not be afraid; do not be discouraged, for the LORD your God will be with you wherever you go. (Joshua 1:9 NIV)

When I was in high school, I hated running the 400-meter, as it was very uncomfortable toward the end of the race. During track meets, I would complain, hide, cry, or do whatever I could to avoid running it. When that didn't work, I ran scared and didn't try my hardest, hoping to avoid the pain. One day, I decided to get over my fear of discomfort and ran my race as fast as I could, and I won! After that, I ran my hardest each time, no matter how bad it made me feel. I made my team's 4x400 relay team, and we eventually won the state title.

Fear can keep people from doing what God has given them the ability to do. We may face scary and uncertain situations, but since God is always with us, we never have to be fearful about the unknown. This commandment that God gave to Joshua thousands of years ago is still true for each of us today. We can be strong and *courageous* in any situation because we know we are never alone.

The next time you

> **WORD FOCUS:**
>
> **courageous** – to be brave while facing fear

are afraid to do something, remember God's promise. He will be with you wherever you go. No matter how scary something may seem, believe you can still be strong and courageous because God is right there with you.

WEEK 34

Have I not commanded you? Be strong and courageous. Do not be afraid; do not be discouraged, for the LORD your God will be with you wherever you go. (Joshua 1:9 NIV)

DAY 1: WARM UP
- ❏ Read this week's verse out loud.
- ❏ Fear is a natural response you may have when facing something new or unknown. How do you usually respond when you are afraid of something or someone?
- ❏ Read the scripture out loud again.
- ❏ Pray for God to speak to you this week about how to respond during scary situations.

DAY 2: BREAK IT DOWN
- ❏ Read this week's verse out loud.
- ❏ Rewrite the scripture in your own words and make it personally about you.
- ❏ Athletes perform exercises during workouts to strengthen

their bodies for competition. Are there any areas in your life you don't feel strong in? What can you work on to get stronger?

❑ Finish your workout by praying for God to help strengthen you in the areas you identified.

DAY 3: GET IN POSITION

❑ Read this week's verse out loud.

❑ In every tough situation, there is always a moment for you to choose fear. God knows you might not feel courageous in certain situations, but He has commanded you to be courageous anyway. What does showing courage mean to you?

❑ Repeat the scripture out loud.

❑ Pray that you will learn how to be courageous, even when you may feel fear.

DAY 4: HUDDLE UP

❑ Read this week's verse out loud.

❑ Discuss with your parent, coach, or other trusted adult about times they have felt afraid about doing something. Discuss how they responded and if they showed courage or fear. Talk about lessons they learned and advice they can give for when you are facing fear.

❑ Pray together that you both would be strong and courageous the next time you face a difficult challenge.

DAY 5: PUSH THROUGH

- ❏ Try to recite this week's verse out loud without looking.
- ❏ Being mentally strong helps you show courage when facing tough situations. Developing courage starts with mental strength. Are there any areas you may sometimes feel mentally weak in? What are some ways you can become mentally strong?
- ❏ Recite this week's scripture again.
- ❏ End by praying that God would strengthen your mind, so you can easily decide to be courageous when needed.

DAY 6: PRACTICE MAKES PERFECT

- ❏ Try again to recite this week's verse out loud. Spend time practicing until you can almost say it from memory.
- ❏ The reason you can be strong and courageous is that God promises to be with you wherever you go. There is never a situation you will find yourself in where God is not there. Thinking back on all you've learned about God from this book, how can this help you have more courage?
- ❏ Pray that you will always remember you are never alone, and that God is always with you.

DAY 7: FINISH STRONG

- ❏ Recite this week's verse. Spend time practicing until you can say it from memory.
- ❏ If I made a different decision at the starting line on that first day, I may have never been a state champion. Your choices

today may affect your future in ways you can't imagine right now. Every time you struggle with courage, remind yourself to be brave for your future. What are future plans that you have, that require you to be courageous now?

❏ Pray that God will continue to help you be strong and courageous so that you will achieve everything He has planned for your life.

❏ Close out this week by saying the scripture from memory.

SIMPLE DELIGHTS

Take delight in the LORD, and he will give you the desires of your heart. (Psalms 37:4 NIV)

Think about the people you spend the most time with. Is it your family? Your friends? Or maybe your teammates? When you enjoy being around someone, you usually feel **delighted** when you are with them and want to spend more time together. When you spend a lot of time with someone, you may start talking and acting the same way, and that might either be a good or bad thing.

The desires of our hearts are those things we want in our lives. This week, we learn that when we take delight in the Lord by enjoying the time we spend with Him, we become more like Him, and He gives us those things that we desire in our hearts.

Building a relationship by spending so much time with God will eventually change us. As we grow closer to Him, we learn more about Him, and our desires will slowly transform into His desires for us. When

WORD FOCUS:

delight – great pleasure

we desire what God desires, He is more than happy to give them to us, as He knows they'll fit right in with His plan for our lives.

WEEK 35

Take delight in the LORD, and he will give you the desires of your heart. (Psalms 37:4 NIV)

DAY 1: WARM UP

❏ Read this week's verse out loud.

❏ Think about the time you spend with God and how you feel about it. Do you enjoy learning about Him or is it more of a bother or hassle?

❏ Read the scripture out loud again.

❏ Pray for God to speak to you this week about the benefits of spending time with Him.

DAY 2: BREAK IT DOWN

❏ Read this week's verse out loud.

❏ Rewrite the scripture in your own words and make it personally about you.

❏ The more time you spend with someone, the more you'll learn about them, and they will also learn more about you. Think about the people you hang out with the most. What kind of influence do they have on what you do, what you say, and where you go?

❏ Finish your workout by praying that God will help you choose the right people to spend time with so that you don't experience negative influences.

DAY 3: GET IN POSITION

❏ Read this week's verse out loud.

❏ People usually enjoy doing things that make them feel good and improve their lives. Think about the things you enjoy doing—maybe your favorite sport, or a hobby. How do you make time to do the things you enjoy? Do you make the same effort to spend time with God?

❏ Repeat the scripture out loud.

❏ Pray that you will get in the habit of making regular time with God that you can enjoy.

DAY 4: HUDDLE UP

❏ Read this week's verse out loud.

❏ Talk to your parent, coach, or other trusted adult about the relationship they have with God. Discuss how and why they spend time with Him, and what they enjoy about it. Also, ask for suggestions for how you can enjoy spending time with God. Write down ideas that you want to try.

❏ Pray together that you both would continue to find ways to enjoy the time you spend with God.

DAY 5: PUSH THROUGH

❏ Try to recite this week's verse out loud without looking.

❏ When a child asks a parent for something, if it will help the child and not harm them, they will usually get what they've asked for. When you spend time with God, you'll learn about things that are good for you, and you'll want them in your life. Think about some things you want in your life. Are there things you want or prayed for that you haven't received?

❑ Recite this week's scripture again.

❑ End by praying that as you spend more time with God, He would show you the desires He has for you.

DAY 6: PRACTICE MAKES PERFECT

❑ Try again to recite this week's verse out loud. Spend time practicing until you can almost say it from memory.

❑ We usually desire things because we think they will make us happy, even though they may not always be good for us. As you spend more time with God, you may notice your desires changing in a good way. Have there been any changes to the desires you had at the beginning of the week?

❑ Pray that as you grow closer to God, you will learn and desire the great plans He has for your life.

DAY 7: FINISH STRONG

❑ Recite this week's verse. Spend time practicing until you can say it from memory.

❑ This week, we learned the benefit of delighting yourself in God. Think about the different ways you can do this. What is one thing you will commit to doing with God that brings you joy?

❑ Pray that your time with God will be filled with joy, and thank Him for granting the desires of your heart.

❑ Close out this week by saying the scripture from memory.

WALKING IN WISDOM

If any of you lacks wisdom, you should ask God, who gives generously to all without finding fault, and it will be given to you.

(James 1:5 NIV)

Knowledge is the information we can learn from being taught, studying on our own, or from life experiences. If you've played the same sport for a long time, then you probably increased your skills and abilities from knowledge through practices, competition, coaching, watching videos, and reading books. But to become a great athlete, it takes more than just knowledge of the game; you must also have the **wisdom** for how to use that knowledge to beat the opponent during competition.

You have been gaining knowledge each week, but it won't be very useful unless you know how to use it. This is where wisdom comes in, and God freely gives it to anyone who asks. Wisdom allows you to make smart decisions throughout your life by putting all the knowledge you've learned into action.

> **WORD FOCUS:**
>
> **wisdom** – having the knowledge or experience needed to make a good decision

We have a way to receive all the wisdom needed to get through difficult situations. All we have to do is ask for it; there is no limit to how much we can have, and there is nothing else we need to do to get it. Whenever we need help making a decision, we can go directly to God for wisdom.

WEEK 36

If any of you lacks wisdom, you should ask God, who gives generously to all without finding fault, and it will be given to you.
(James 1:5 NIV)

DAY 1: WARM UP

❑ Read this week's verse out loud.

❑ As we go through life, there are many decisions we must make. This week's scripture helps you whenever you are in a situation and don't know what to do. Think about the last major decision you had to make—maybe it was related to school, sports, hobbies, friends, or family. Write down all the steps you took to decide what to do.

❑ Read the scripture out loud again.

❑ Pray that God will show you how to receive wisdom from Him when you need help in making a decision.

DAY 2: BREAK IT DOWN

❏ Read this week's verse out loud.

❏ Rewrite the scripture in your own words and make it personally about you.

❏ Some people don't understand the difference between knowledge and wisdom. Knowledge is what you know, and wisdom is how you use what you know. When you are unsure of what to do, God can help you use the knowledge you have to make the right choices in your life. Think about a choice you have to make now, or in the future. What knowledge will you use to help you decide?

❏ Finish your workout asking God to help you with the knowledge you have to make a wise decision.

DAY 3: GET IN POSITION

❏ Read this week's verse out loud.

❏ A fool is someone who is not wise. A foolish person does not show good judgment while making choices. They may not think things through before making a decision, or they may make a choice that goes against the knowledge they have, which usually leads to a bad outcome. Have you ever made a decision you knew wasn't right but made it anyway? What happened as a result of your choice?

❏ Repeat the scripture out loud.

❏ Pray that God would keep you from making foolish decisions, so you don't have to experience the consequences of bad choices.

DAY 4: HUDDLE UP

❑ Read this week's verse out loud.

❑ Ask your parent, coach, or other trusted adult for their definition of wisdom. Discuss why having wisdom is so important as a young person, as there are many decisions to make that will impact your future. Ask them to talk about the areas they have gained wisdom in over the years.

❑ Pray together that you will use wisdom to make decisions that are important for your future.

DAY 5: PUSH THROUGH

❑ Try to recite this week's verse out loud without looking.

❑ When we ask God for wisdom, He gives it generously. This means God will never run out; there is always more wisdom available for you. You can have as much as you need; all you have to do is ask.

❑ Recite this week's scripture again.

❑ End today by praying that you will always have the courage to ask God for more wisdom when you need it, instead of trying to figure things out on your own.

DAY 6: PRACTICE MAKES PERFECT

❑ Try again to recite this week's verse out loud. Spend time practicing until you can almost say it from memory.

❑ A past record of bad choices does not affect God's choice to give wisdom to anyone who asks for it. He will not look for reasons you should not have wisdom, and there is nothing you can do that will keep you from receiving it. You just have to ask. Do you sometimes feel like bad choices you've made will keep you from God's blessings? Explain why or why not.

❑ Pray that God will remind you that He is always there, and always willing to give you wisdom, no matter what you've done in the past.

DAY 7: FINISH STRONG

❑ Recite this week's verse. Spend time practicing until you can say it from memory.

❑ You've learned a lot of information in this book and gotten new knowledge. Wisdom will show you how to use that knowledge to make decisions and choices for the rest of your life. As you get older, you may find yourself in a situation where you don't know which choice to make. Continue to ask God for wisdom as it will always be available to you. Do you ever feel like you must make decisions alone, and don't have enough information? How can God and other wise friends and family help you?

❑ Pray that you will always be a wise person, by receiving wisdom from God when you need it.

❑ Close out this week by saying the scripture from memory.

PROTECT YOUR HOUSE

Guard your heart above all else, for it determines the course of your life. (Proverbs 4:23 NLT)

The role of the defense is to prevent the offense from scoring. There are some situations you can plan and prepare for, while other defensive moves require a quick response. There may not always be time to fully think through your defensive response before making it, but the goal is always to stop your opponent any way you can.

In life, we are the defenders of our thoughts and emotions. We must work hard to keep Satan from scoring in the goal of our minds. We have to **guard** our hearts against any kind of attack because our thoughts control our actions, and our actions will impact our future. Every attack on our hearts and minds is meant to knock us off the path God has put us on.

There are messages, images, thoughts, and ideas coming at us nonstop, especially through other people and technology. Think about what your mind is being exposed to through friends, movies, songs, and books. You must guard your mind against all harmful messages and defend it well. Your life

> **WORD FOCUS:**
>
> **guard** – protect against harm

depends on it.

WEEK 37

Guard your heart above all else, for it determines the course of your life. (Proverbs 4:23 NLT)

DAY 1: WARM UP

❏ Read this week's verse out loud.

❏ Your heart described in this week's verse is not the organ pumping blood to your body, but it's referring to your thoughts, emotions, and desires that are connected to your mind. What do you think 'protecting your heart' means?

❏ Read the scripture out loud again.

❏ Pray for God to show you why it's important to guard your heart.

DAY 2: BREAK IT DOWN

❏ Read this week's verse out loud.

❏ Rewrite the scripture in your own words and make it personally about you.

❏ Think about some of the things that have access to your mind—some examples are social media, television, radio, movies, streaming, books, and video games. Write down the impact these sources have on your mind, whether positive or negative.

❏ Pray that you would be aware of what you allow in your mind and how it affects you.

DAY 3: GET IN POSITION

❏ Read this week's verse out loud.

❏ Your heart experiences a lot of emotions. Your thoughts can lead to positive feelings like happiness, joy, excitement, and hope; or they can cause difficult feelings like anger, hopelessness, jealousy, and disappointment. All these feelings can affect the choices and decisions you make. What are some ways that your feelings have affected your choices? How might choices based on feelings affect your future?

❏ Repeat the scripture out loud.

❏ Pray that you would be aware of how your feelings are affecting your choices so they don't negatively affect your future.

DAY 4: HUDDLE UP

❏ Read this week's verse out loud.

❏ Discuss with your parent, coach, or other trusted adult the importance of guarding your heart. Talk about the list you made on Day 2 and discuss ways you can protect your mind against negative thoughts and feelings that might impact your future. Ask for suggestions and write down how you can defend your mind against each item on your list.

❑ Pray together that God will show you how to how to guard your mind against attacks that can affect your future.

DAY 5: PUSH THROUGH

❑ Try to recite this week's verse out loud without looking.

❑ To guard your heart, you must know how the enemy wants to attack you. We previously learned that Satan's strategy is to kill, steal, and destroy. How can protecting your mind defend you against his plan?

❑ Recite this week's scripture again.

❑ End by praying that you will remain on guard and be aware of Satan's tricks to attack your heart.

DAY 6: PRACTICE MAKES PERFECT

❑ Try again to recite this week's verse out loud. Spend time practicing until you can almost say it from memory.

❑ Suicide and depression rates are at an all-time high. When the mind is being attacked with more negative thoughts than it can handle, it may not know how to respond properly. How can you train your mind to be aware of when the pressure is too much for you to handle by yourself?

❑ Pray for strategies on responding to tough thoughts and feelings before they can overtake your heart.

DAY 7: FINISH STRONG

❑ Recite this week's verse. Spend time practicing until you can say it from memory.

❑ Not following this week's scripture can affect your life and future—either in a good way or a bad one. It all depends on how well you take care of your heart. The words "above all else" in the verse show how important it is to follow this advice. Why do you think guarding your heart is one of the most important things you can do for your future?

❑ Pray that you will never let your guard down when it comes to your heart and that you will always be careful about what you allow into your mind from any source, including social media, television, radio, movies, streaming, books, and video games.

❑ Close out this week by saying the scripture from memory.

Section 7:

WHAT ARE MY PROMISES?

LET GO OF THE PAST

So now there is no condemnation for those who belong to Christ Jesus. (Romans 8:1 NLT)

In *The Lion King*, Simba experienced a tragedy he believed was his fault, which caused him to run away from home in shame. As a result, he grew up without his family. He eventually learned there was nothing he could do about the past, except learn from it. Eventually, he ran back home and changed his future.

Condemnation can cause someone to feel terrible about something they have done, regardless of the reason. As Believers, we should not feel shame about our past, because Jesus died for all the sins we've ever committed. When we ask for forgiveness, we're simply forgiven, and there's no reason to feel bad or bring it up again. His forgiveness allows us to let go of our past.

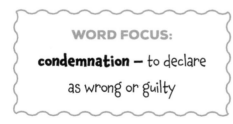

WORD FOCUS:

condemnation – to declare as wrong or guilty

It's important that we learn from the past, but don't live in it. When there's no condemnation, we are free from the guilt and shame of anything we've ever done. No matter how often we mess up, we can always pick ourselves up, dust ourselves off, and keep moving forward. Don't remain stuck in the past.

WEEK 38

So now there is no condemnation for those who belong to Christ Jesus. (Romans 8:1 NLT)

DAY 1: WARM UP

❑ Read this week's verse out loud.

❑ You learned in Week 26 that every person on earth has sinned. Have you done something in the past you can't forgive yourself for?

❑ Read the scripture out loud again.

❑ Pray for God to speak to you this week about anything in your past you need to let go of.

DAY 2: BREAK IT DOWN

❑ Read this week's verse out loud.

❑ Rewrite the scripture in your own words and make it personally about you.

❑ You also learned in Week 25 that you have an accuser who wants to point out everything you've done wrong. But you also learned that Jesus died to forgive you for everything bad that you've done. How can you ignore the accuser when he tries to make you feel guilty about your past?

❑ Pray that when you start to feel guilty about your past, you'll know those feelings are from the accuser and that you will be able to ignore him.

DAY 3: GET IN POSITION

❑ Read this week's verse out loud.

❑ If you've asked Jesus to live inside your heart and forgive your sins, then you are forgiven, even though you still may feel bad about something you have done. How do you know you are forgiven?

❑ Repeat the scripture out loud.

❑ Pray that you remember that Jesus took your sins with Him on the cross and forgives you as soon as you ask.

DAY 4: HUDDLE UP

❑ Read this week's verse out loud.

❑ Discuss with your parent, coach, or other trusted adult about anything they may have done in the past that they still feel bad about. Talk about how being stuck in the past can keep you from moving ahead in your future. Come up with ways that each of you can get unstuck.

❑ Pray together that God will show you how to move forward, instead of being stuck in the past.

DAY 5: PUSH THROUGH

❑ Try to recite this week's verse out loud without looking.

❑ After you've asked Jesus for forgiveness, you must forgive yourself and be ready to let the past go and move on. If there is someone you have hurt, you must ask for their forgiveness as well. Write down steps you will take to ask someone else for forgiveness and also to forgive yourself.

❑ Recite this week's scripture again.

❑ Pray that you will have the courage to ask for forgiveness from anyone you may have hurt with your words or actions.

DAY 6: PRACTICE MAKES PERFECT

❑ Try again to recite this week's verse out loud. Spend time practicing until you can almost say it from memory.

❑ There's no way to change what happened in the past, and not letting go can leave you trapped in a cage of guilt and embarrassment. If you continue to struggle, keep forgiving yourself and remember God says you are not guilty. Is there something you've done that you are having a hard time forgiving yourself for? Does something you've done in the past still bother you?

❑ End by praying that you will be able to follow the example from Jesus and forgive yourself for anything you've done but haven't been able to let go of.

DAY 7: FINISH STRONG

❑ Recite this week's verse. Spend time practicing until you can say it from memory.

❑ Jesus died on the cross so that anything bad you've ever done could be forgiven, and that once you've accepted Him into your life, you've become a new person. Becoming a new person means leaving the past behind you. Every day you live, your past is moving further behind you. What do you think your life will look like if you never felt guilt again?

❑ Pray that you will remember you are a new person and that once you ask for forgiveness, you can leave the past behind you.

❑ Close out this week by saying the scripture from memory.

HOLD ON UNTIL MORNING

Weeping may last through the night, but joy comes with the morning. (Psalms 30:5 NLT)

If you look at the faces of the losing team after a championship game, you may see tears—even from the biggest, strongest, scariest players. At some point, we all may experience disappointment, pain, or loss, and crying is a natural response to the physical or emotional pain those experiences can bring.

We face tough times in life because sin exists in the world. Sin brings painful situations that can happen to anyone. No matter how good a person is, bad things may still affect them. We may cry due to the pain we feel, but the tears won't last forever. Because Jesus died for us, He can heal any pain we may feel. That healing may come by the next morning, or it may take days, weeks, months, or even years for joy to come back.

> **WORD FOCUS:**
>
> **weeping** – crying

We cry when we are feeling the loss of something—maybe a hope or a dream, or a loss that has taken something from your life. It's important to allow space for sadness and time to work through those feelings. Pain will not last forever as it will end eventually, but we don't always know when. You just have to stay strong until your morning comes.

WEEK 39

Weeping may last through the night, but joy comes with the morning. (Psalms 30:5 NLT)

DAY 1: WARM UP

❑ Read this week's verse out loud.

❑ There are many reasons people cry. Write down the last time you cried and why. How did you feel afterward?

❑ Read the scripture out loud again.

❑ Pray for God to show you how you can give your tears and the things that make you cry over to Him.

DAY 2: BREAK IT DOWN

❑ Read this week's verse out loud.

❑ Rewrite the scripture in your own words and make it personally about you.

❑ The morning brings a new day, and with it hope. Have you ever gone to bed worried about something, only to think clearly about it in the morning? Why do you think mornings bring change?

❑ Pray that every morning you wake up, you will be filled

with hope.

DAY 3: GET IN POSITION

❑ Read this week's verse out loud.

❑ Pain, whether it is physical, emotional, or mental, can cause tears. When your body is in pain, or your feelings have been hurt, or there's a thought in your mind that you can't seem to push out, a natural response may be to cry. What are some other ways you can respond?

❑ Repeat the scripture out loud.

❑ Pray that you'll learn positive ways to deal with pain in your life.

DAY 4: HUDDLE UP

❑ Read this week's verse out loud.

❑ Talk with your parent, coach, or other trusted adult about the last time they experienced a tough situation that made them cry. Discuss how things turned out in the end, and if the morning brought them joy. Discuss the difference between joy and happiness. Does this scripture mean you will always be happy in the morning?

❑ Pray together that you will be strong and know that your tears will stop one day, and you will eventually experience joy instead of pain.

Day 5: PUSH THROUGH

❑ Try to recite this week's verse out loud without looking.

❑ Sometimes it may feel like a tough situation will never end, which can bring on feelings of hopelessness and depression. If you or someone you know is having these feelings, how might you use this week's scripture to fight those thoughts and emotions?

❑ Recite this week's scripture again.

❑ Pray that you will never lose hope while going through tough situations.

DAY 6: PRACTICE MAKES PERFECT

❑ Try again to recite this week's verse out loud. Spend time practicing until you can almost say it from memory.

❑ The word morning in this scripture does not always mean the next day or even the early part of the day. Morning represents the start of something new, which brings change and hope. Your morning is when God changes your situation. How will you know when your morning has arrived? What are you praying for God to change?

❑ Pray that God will help you to be strong while you wait for your morning to come.

DAY 7: FINISH STRONG

❑ Recite this week's verse. Spend time practicing until you can say it from memory.

❑ As you close out this week, picture a morning sunrise: the first view of light comes when the sun is first visible and keeps getting brighter until it fills the entire sky. It is the beginning of a new day, new opportunities, and new choices. Do you look forward to each new day? How does watching a sunrise make you feel?

❑ Pray that every time you see a sunrise, you will be reminded it's a new day filled with hope, and the past is behind you.

❑ Close out this week by saying the scripture from memory.

EVERYTHING IS TAKEN CARE OF

And my God shall supply all your **need** according to His riches in glory by Jesus Christ. (Philippians 4:19 NKJV)

Food, clothes, and a place to live are the basic needs of life. A parent or caregiver must provide at least these things for a helpless baby to survive. As a child grows older, new physical, mental, and emotional needs are discovered. There are things we can provide for ourselves, but there are needs we must also depend on others for.

Like a good parent, God won't let us go without anything we truly need. Since everything ultimately belongs to Him, there's nothing He can't provide for us. And because God created us, He knows what we need at any moment in time. Through our relationship with Jesus Christ, we can trust that our needs will always be met.

> **WORD FOCUS:**
>
> **need** – something that is required or very important

We should be thankful for all God has blessed us with, but we should not expect Him to give us everything we want. He's not a magic wizard waiting to grant our wishes. Some things we pray for may not be good for us or may not go along with His plan for our lives. But we can always trust Him to provide all that we need.

WEEK 40

And my God shall supply all your need according to His riches in glory by Jesus Christ. (Philippians 4:19 NKJV)

DAY 1: WARM UP

❑ Read this week's verse out loud.

❑ In Week 3, you learned that God is your Shepherd and provides for you. He knows everything about you and wants to take care of you. Write down any prayer requests for what you need today.

❑ Read the scripture out loud again.

❑ Tell God about your prayer request. Ask for what you need God to do in your life.

DAY 2: BREAK IT DOWN

❑ Read this week's verse out loud.

❑ Rewrite the scripture in your own words and make it personally about you.

❑ You have physical needs like eating healthy foods and getting a good night's sleep, and mental needs like understanding your schoolwork and knowing how to make good decisions.

You also have emotional needs like forming strong, positive relationships with friends, family, and teammates. How do you depend on God to help you with all those needs?

❏ Pray that you will trust God to provide for you in each area of your life.

DAY 3: GET IN POSITION

❏ Read this week's verse out loud.
❏ There are many things you can do on your own, and you may not include God in them, but He wants you to involve Him in every part of your life. Even when you feel like you don't need God's help, always include Him anyway. What is an area of your life that you've been handling on your own?
❏ Repeat the scripture out loud.
❏ Pray and invite God into that area you wrote down. Invite Him into that part of your life and ask for His help.

DAY 4: HUDDLE UP

❏ Read this week's verse out loud.
❏ Discuss with your parent, coach, or other trusted adult about knowing the difference between wants and needs. Discuss how to deal with the disappointment of not always getting what you want. How can the knowledge that God will provide what you need help you deal with not always getting what you want?
❏ Pray together that you will trust God enough to be okay when you don't get want you want from Him.

DAY 5: PUSH THROUGH

❏ Try to recite this week's verse out loud without looking.

❏ There are needs we have no control over, like the sunshine and rain. God has control over everything in the world, so He will never run out of anything you need. How can remembering this help you the next time you worry about something you don't have but feel like you need?

❏ Recite this week's scripture again.

❏ Pray that you will always remember that God has the power to provide whatever you need, and if you don't have something important you've been praying for, it simply means you don't need it...yet.

DAY 6: PRACTICE MAKES PERFECT

❏ Try again to recite this week's verse out loud. Spend time practicing until you can almost say it from memory.

❏ God also wants you to help others, by giving your time and help to someone else that needs it. When God sees you helping someone else, He is even more motivated to help you. Can you think of a family member, friend, classmate, or teammate that needs help? What can you do to help them?

❏ Pray that God will show you ways you can help others around you, and that you will always be willing to help.

DAY 7: FINISH STRONG

❏ Recite this week's verse. Spend time practicing until you

can say it from memory.

- ❏ You can trust God for everything you need to live your life for Him. You may not have everything you want, but you can be sure that you have everything you need. God provides us everything we need through Jesus. Why do you think everything we need must come through Jesus?
- ❏ Thank God that you can trust in His never-ending supply of riches through Jesus Christ to bless your life.
- ❏ Close out this week by saying the scripture from memory.

NO NEED TO FIGHT

The LORD will fight for you; you need only to be still.

(Exodus 14:14 NIV)

'Fight or Flight' describes the response someone has when they are in danger. Our brain directs our body to either run away (flight) or fight off the danger. When we find ourselves in a **desperate** situation, we may feel trapped and start to panic, and may respond without thinking.

When Moses and the children of Israel left slavery in Egypt, they eventually were blocked by the Red Sea in front of them, with Pharaoh's army behind them. When the people started to panic, Moses knew not to be afraid, because God was with them. He trusted that God would fight for them and told the people to be still. God responded by separating the water so the people could walk through the sea on dry land, saving them from their enemies.

> **WORD FOCUS:**
>
> **desperate** – extremely bad, serious, or dangerous

When you face a hopeless situation, instead of fighting or running away, the correct response is to be still and trust God. Being still doesn't mean stand by and do nothing. It means trusting God, reading your Bible, and praying about the situation, while allowing God to fight and win your battles.

WEEK 41

The LORD will fight for you; you need only to be still.
(Exodus 14:14 NIV)

DAY 1: WARM UP

❑ Read this week's verse out loud.

❑ 'Fight or Flight' is a common response in an urgent situation, but there are other ways to respond. How do you usually respond when you are in a desperate situation?

❑ Read the scripture out loud again.

❑ Pray that you will understand how you should respond in stressful or difficult situations.

DAY 2: BREAK IT DOWN

❑ Read this week's verse out loud.

❑ Rewrite the scripture in your own words and make it personally about you.

❑ When facing a desperate situation, God wants you to trust Him instead of coming up with your own plan. Psalms 46:10 tells you to "Be still and know that I am God." As you think about all you have learned about God while reading this book, how can that help you trust Him to handle your situation?

❏ Pray that you will remember how great and powerful God is when facing a difficult situation.

DAY 3: GET IN POSITION

❏ Read this week's verse out loud.

❏ When you notice yourself growing anxious or fearful, instead of coming up with a plan on your own, think back to what you learned in Week 33. Stop and follow the steps: Pray, Ask, and Thank. After you have done this, it will be much easier for you to be still and wait for God to respond. Write down the steps from Week 33 and how you plan to use them.

❏ Repeat the scripture out loud.

❏ Pray that when facing a desperate situation, you would remember to follow the steps you learned—to pray to God about what's going on, ask for what you want God to do, and then thank Him for handling the situation.

DAY 4: HUDDLE UP

❏ Read this week's verse out loud.

❏ Discuss with your parent, coach, or other trusted adult about how responding without thinking could make things even worse for you. Ask them to share a time when they responded to a situation without thinking it through and the outcome. What are the dangers of responding without thinking?

❑ Pray together that you would not respond without thinking your actions through.

DAY 5: PUSH THROUGH

❑ Try to recite this week's verse out loud without looking.

❑ Sometimes situations that look hopeless may cause us to do something that will make things more difficult. But even if you did something to make a situation worse, this week's strategy can still be followed. You can stop trying to figure out what to do at any time, hand your situation over to God and be still. Is there anything you are dealing with right now that you need to give to God?

❑ Recite this week's scripture again.

❑ Pray about your situation and tell God about it, so you can hand it over to Him.

DAY 6: PRACTICE MAKES PERFECT

❑ Try again to recite this week's verse out loud. Spend time practicing until you can almost say it from memory.

❑ When Moses led the children of Israel out of Egypt, they faced a desperate situation. Going forward into the sea would have caused them to drown, and fighting the army behind them would have brought certain death and defeat. Being still allowed God to save them by doing something they could not do for themselves. When something seems really bad, what steps can you take to calm yourself down and trust God to fight for you?

❑ Pray that you would remember to trust God when things look desperate and to remember there is nothing or no one more powerful than Him.

DAY 7: FINISH STRONG

❑ Recite this week's verse. Spend time practicing until you can say it from memory.

❑ By using this week's strategy, you no longer have to figure out how to solve your problems. You have been learning all the amazing things about God as you've read through this book and now it's time to trust Him. What have you learned about being still this week? How and when will you be still in the future?

❑ Thank God for teaching you to be still and trust Him while He fights your battles.

❑ Close out this week by saying the scripture from memory.

USELESS AND DEFECTIVE

No weapon formed against you shall prosper.

(Isaiah 54:17a NKJV)

Coaches may watch or spy on other teams they are scheduled to play against, to get information about their plays, identify their best players, and determine their strengths and weaknesses. This is to help coaches design a game plan to beat their opponents.

You are also being spied on by your enemy, so he can make plans and design tricks to use as weapons against you. A weapon is a tool used to **inflict** harm or damage. We are promised that no matter how painful they feel, and no matter how much damage they seem to cause, none of Satan's weapons will ever succeed against us.

WORD FOCUS:

inflict – to cause or bring

Once you decide to live for the Lord, you will face hard times and attacks from your enemy. He will do everything in his power to make you give up. His weapons may hurt you and cause you to slip or fall down, but always remember no matter what you may face, those weapons will never beat or defeat you.

WEEK 42

No weapon formed against you shall prosper.

(Isaiah 54:17a NKJV)

DAY 1: WARM UP

❑ Read this week's verse out loud.

❑ A weapon is something designed to cause harm or damage. It can be used against you physically, emotionally, or mentally. Throughout this book, you have learned information about an enemy that wants to harm you. What kind of weapons do you think Satan used on you in the past?

❑ Read the scripture out loud again.

❑ Pray that you will be on the lookout for weapons that may be used against you by your enemy.

DAY 2: BREAK IT DOWN

❑ Read this week's verse out loud.

❑ Rewrite the scripture in your own words and make it personally about you.

❑ It's important to know that weapons will be formed against you, and they might cause you pain. When you are going through a painful situation, how does this scripture remind you that everything will be okay?

❑ Pray that you will remember when you are going through a

painful situation, things will work out in the end.

DAY 3: GET IN POSITION

❏ Read this week's verse out loud.
❏ In an earlier section of this book, you learned some strategies your spiritual enemy uses to try to defeat you. Do you remember any of those tricks Satan uses? How could they be used as weapons to harm you?
❏ Repeat the scripture out loud.
❏ Pray that you are aware of the weapons Satan tries to use against you so that you will be prepared to respond.

DAY 4: HUDDLE UP

❏ Read this week's verse out loud.
❏ Discuss with your parent, coach, or other trusted adult about tough situations you may be going through. Ask them to share a situation where they faced a tough time and thought it was not going to end well, but it turned out okay. Ask for advice on what you can do while going through difficult times. Write down any ideas you would like to try.
❏ Pray together that you will find ways to be strong as you go through tough times.

DAY 5: PUSH THROUGH

❏ Try to recite this week's verse out loud without looking.
❏ If it feels like the same trick keeps causing you problems in your life, it may be because Satan has found a weapon he

thinks will work on you. As you say today's scripture, think about that situation. Write down what you will do so you don't fall for it next time.

❑ Recite this week's scripture again.

❑ End by praying that God will help you to finally overcome something that has been hard to beat in the past.

DAY 6: PRACTICE MAKES PERFECT

❑ Try again to recite this week's verse out loud. Spend time practicing until you can almost say it from memory.

❑ Even though weapons may not prosper, they may still bring pain. Sometimes the pain may come in the form of sadness, frustration, anger, depression, or helplessness. This pain can sometimes cause you to make bad choices in an attempt to feel better. If you are dealing with any pain, is there a better way you can deal with it, now that you know it won't beat you?

❑ Pray that God will allow you to respond the right way when you are feeling pain from a weapon.

DAY 7: FINISH STRONG

❑ Recite this week's verse. Spend time practicing until you can say it from memory.

❑ You may even need time and help to recover from the pain you experienced but remember that your story will always end with healing and victory. How will knowing this good news help you get through tough times?

- ❏ Thank God for His promise that no weapon formed against you will succeed.
- ❏ Close out this week by saying the scripture from memory.

INVINCIBLE GOD

If God is for us, who can ever be against us? (Romans 8:31 NLT)

Everyone seems to love a David vs. Goliath sports story. There have been countless movies where a person or team faced a bigger opponent, where it seems they had no chance of winning. But then, by some miracle, the stronger opponent gets beaten by the weaker one.

In the original story, David faced the bigger and more powerful Goliath with only five stones, instead of the regular armor that was used in battle. By doing this, he showed complete confidence in God's ability to protect him in the fight against Goliath. Before David threw the stone to kill Goliath, he declared, "I come to you in the name of the Lord!"

When you are facing a giant in your life and it feels like there's no way you can possibly win, think back to David's confidence in God. David showed he trusted the power of God by facing Goliath and throwing the stone. Then God did the rest. When facing situations that feel too big for you to overcome, remember who you have on your side and be confident that nothing or no one will ever be able to defeat you.

WEEK 43

If God is for us, who can ever be against us? (Romans 8:31 NLT)

DAY 1: WARM UP

- ❑ Read this week's verse out loud.
- ❑ If someone is "for you", it means they help and support you. Think of some people that are for you. How do their care and support help you?
- ❑ Read the scripture out loud again.
- ❑ Pray that God would show you all the support you have in your life.

DAY 2: BREAK IT DOWN

- ❑ Read this week's verse out loud.
- ❑ Rewrite the scripture in your own words and make it personally about you.
- ❑ When someone is against you, they don't want you to succeed. You already know you have an enemy that is against you. You may also have people in your life that want you to fail. How does it make you feel knowing that people may be against you?
- ❑ Thank God that He is for you, no matter who is against you.

DAY 3: GET IN POSITION

❏ Read this week's verse out loud.

❏ Everyone in David's army was afraid of Goliath, but David showed confidence in the power of God. David knew that God kept him safe from danger when he was a shepherd, so he trusted Him in an even more dangerous situation. Think about a time when God protected you. How does remembering what God has done in the past help you trust Him in the future?

❏ Repeat the scripture out loud.

❏ Pray that you will always remember God's protection in the past so you will trust Him when facing new challenges.

DAY 4: HUDDLE UP

❏ Read this week's verse out loud.

❏ Discuss with your parent, coach, or other trusted adult why they are "for you". Discuss specific areas you need help and support with, whether it's school, relationships, sports, or another issue. Share how they can help you and ask for any advice they may have. Write down any action steps you want to take after the conversation.

❏ Thank God for all the support He has given you in your life.

DAY 5: PUSH THROUGH

❏ Try to recite this week's verse out loud without looking.

❏ Goliath was considered one of the greatest warriors of his time. Even though David was smaller and less experienced in fighting, he still beat Goliath. It wasn't because there was anything special about David, it was because he confidently trusted in God's power. Can you trust God when facing a situation that seems too big for you to handle?

❑ Recite this week's scripture again.

❑ End by praying you will have confidence in God's power to help you against the "giant" situations in your life.

DAY 6: PRACTICE MAKES PERFECT

❑ Try again to recite this week's verse out loud. Spend time practicing until you can almost say it from memory.

❑ God's power and greatness are shown throughout the Bible. There is no situation or problem that is too great for Him, or that He can't handle. How can you face any "giant" problems in your life when you remember the great and powerful God is helping and supporting you?

❑ Pray that whenever you are facing a giant, you would remember God always has your back.

DAY 7: FINISH STRONG

❑ Recite this week's verse. Spend time practicing until you can say it from memory.

❑ When facing a major situation, remember God will always be greater. David knew no matter how big Goliath appeared to be, God was bigger. After this week, what lessons have you learned from the story of David and Goliath? How will this help you in the future?

❑ Thank God that He is for you and that He will always be greater than anything you may face.

❑ Close out this week by saying the scripture from memory.

NO NEED FOR FEAR

For God has not given us a spirit of fear, but of power and of love and of a sound mind. (2 Timothy 1:7 NKJV)

As an athlete, you've probably faced fear many times. During a tryout, season opener, playoff game, or when facing an undefeated opponent, you may have experienced a combination of worry, nervousness, or anxiety. When you're not sure about something that may happen in your future, those thoughts can often lead to fear.

God has given us three tools to fight fear. The Holy Spirit gives us the power to overcome fear through faith by believing all the promises God has given us. Love comes from God, so when we are fighting fearful thoughts, we can remember how much He loves us, and be assured He'll take care of us. A *sound mind* gives us the ability to make good decisions in difficult situations, instead of making bad decisions by not thinking clearly.

> **WORD FOCUS:**
>
> **sound mind** – mind under control

Satan tries to trick our minds with desperate situations, hoping it will lead to fear and despair. He wants us to respond in a way that will negatively affect our future. When we use the combination of power, love, and a sound mind, we can beat fear every time, and destroy Satan's master weapon against us.

WEEK 44

For God has not given us a spirit of fear, but of power and of love and of a sound mind. (2 Timothy 1:7 NKJV)

DAY 1: WARM UP

- ❏ Read this week's verse out loud.
- ❏ Many people are more concerned about the future, instead of what's going on in the present. How often do you think about your future? Do those thoughts ever cause you to fear what may come?
- ❏ Read the scripture out loud again.
- ❏ Pray for God to speak to you about the weapons He's given you to fight against fear.

DAY 2: BREAK IT DOWN

- ❏ Read this week's verse out loud.
- ❏ Rewrite the scripture in your own words and make it personally about you.
- ❏ You've learned throughout this book that fear is one of the

main weapons Satan tries to use against you, but you've also learned how powerful God is. How can remembering all the scriptures, instructions, and promises you have learned give you the power to fight fear?

❑ Pray that you will understand the power you have through the Holy Spirit.

DAY 3: GET IN POSITION

❑ Read this week's verse out loud.

❑ In Week 15 , we learned about the power we have through the Holy Spirit. Go back and read that section as a reminder of the power inside of you. Write down ways that power can help you fight fear.

❑ Repeat the scripture out loud.

❑ Pray that you always remember to use the power inside of you to fight against any fear you may face.

DAY 4: HUDDLE UP

❑ Read this week's verse out loud.

❑ Throughout the Bible, there are instructions not to fear. Discuss with your parent, coach, or other trusted adult how knowing that God loves you can help you fight off fear. What does it mean to be loved by God? How does His love protect you?

❑ Thank God for His love that allows you to trust in Him during scary situations.

DAY 5: PUSH THROUGH

- ❏ Try to recite this week's verse out loud without looking.
- ❏ Having a sound mind means you are not easily moved by what you see or hear and that you use wisdom before responding to tough situations. How do you respond to things when you are worried or afraid? Are you able to think clearly, or do your emotions take over your mind?
- ❏ Recite this week's scripture again.
- ❏ Pray that you will keep a sound mind when you notice your feelings are affecting your thoughts and actions.

DAY 6: PRACTICE MAKES PERFECT

- ❏ Try again to recite this week's verse out loud. Spend time practicing until you can almost say it from memory.
- ❏ Fear is a tool Satan uses to defeat you. You have power through the Holy Spirit and love through your heavenly Father, which allows you to have a sound mind when facing difficult times in life. How can you use power, love, and a sound mind to fight off fearful thoughts?
- ❏ Pray that God will teach you how to use power, love, and a sound mind together to fight off fear.

DAY 7: FINISH STRONG

- ❏ Recite this week's verse. Spend time practicing until you can say it from memory.
- ❏ There are so many things happening in the world that make it easy to feel worried or afraid. God has given you weapons

to help you fight off fear. You must continue to use them against the attacks of the enemy, as Satan will always try to use fear against you.

❑ Pray that you will get stronger every time you use power, love, and a sound mind against fearful thoughts.

❑ Close out this week by saying the scripture from memory.

A GUARANTEED WIN

Every child of God can defeat the world, and our faith is what gives us this victory. (1 John 5:4 CEV)

We play sports for the love of the game, but we also want to beat our opponent. What if you knew in advance you would win every sporting event that you competed in? That no matter what competition you entered, you would be victorious.

In life we will face greater challenges than what we face on the athletic field. But no matter how tough things may seem, if we don't lose faith that God is in control, we will win our battles. We must never forget that God has carefully planned out our entire lives, and He knows everything about what we are facing, no matter how big or small. Our heavenly Father will always take care of His children.

Even when we feel like the situation is just too big and hard, if we keep our faith and don't give up, we will be victorious. Winning doesn't mean everything will work out the way we want, but it will work out the way it's supposed to, which is the way God planned. Even when we don't understand, we must still trust Him.

WEEK 45

Every child of God can defeat the world, and our faith is what gives us this victory. (1 John 5:4 CEV)

DAY 1: WARM UP

- ❑ Read this week's verse out loud.
- ❑ As an athlete, you probably have faced some tough competition. You might have experienced nervousness or butterflies in your stomach before your game or match. Why do you think you feel that way before you compete?
- ❑ Read the scripture out loud again.
- ❑ Pray that you will understand victory and faith are connected.

DAY 2: BREAK IT DOWN

- ❑ Read this week's verse out loud.
- ❑ Rewrite the scripture in your own words and make it personally about you.
- ❑ One of the exciting things about watching sports is not knowing the outcome. Athletes are competing against each other, hoping to be the winner in the end. If you went into a game or competition knowing you would win, how would that affect your confidence?
- ❑ Pray that God will show you why you can confidently face

every challenge you face.

DAY 3: GET IN POSITION

❑ Read this week's verse out loud.

❑ As a child of God, you must believe in His Son Jesus and receive Him in your life. This is the only way to receive the promise in this week's scripture. This allows you to defeat anything you face. Have you asked Jesus to be your Savior? If not, what's holding you back?

❑ Repeat the scripture out loud.

❑ Thank God for inviting you to be His child through Jesus Christ.

DAY 4: HUDDLE UP

❑ Read this week's verse out loud.

❑ As a child of God, you can defeat the world. Discuss with your parent, coach, or other trusted adult about what the "world" is. After your discussion, think about what it means for you to overcome situations you may face, and write down ways you can defeat the world.

❑ Pray together that you will be prepared for any situation you face from the world.

DAY 5: PUSH THROUGH

❑ Try to recite this week's verse out loud without looking.

❑ As you face tough situations in life, faith is also required to win your battles. Think back to what you learned about faith in Week 30. Even when it doesn't look like it, God has given you the power to beat whatever it is you are going through. How can your faith give you the confidence to face what you're dealing with, knowing you will be victorious in the end?

❏ Recite this week's scripture again.

❏ Pray that you will stand strong in your faith to be able to defeat anything that comes your way.

DAY 6: PRACTICE MAKES PERFECT

❏ Try again to recite this week's verse out loud. Spend time practicing until you can almost say it from memory.

❏ Situations you face may be extremely difficult both physically and emotionally, and may even cause you pain at times. God knows everything going on in your life and has a plan for your victory. Do you trust God enough to help you with your problems, or do some things just seem too big to beat?

❏ Pray that you will trust in God's power to help you and that you will never give up on tough situations.

DAY 7: FINISH STRONG

❏ Recite this week's verse. Spend time practicing until you can say it from memory.

❏ This week, choose to confidently face your struggles— even if they last longer or feel harder than you've ever experienced before. Remember you are a child of God, and be sure your actions show you are trusting God as you deal with your issues. How can you walk by faith when you are facing tough times? What can you do to show what you believe about the outcome?

❑ Thank God for giving His children the ability to overcome and beat anything. Pray that His children will understand the power they have inside.

❑ Close out this week by saying the scripture from memory.

IT WILL ALL WORK OUT

And we know that God causes everything to work together for the good of those who love God and are called according to his purpose for them. (Romans 8:28 NLT)

My daughter experienced a major injury to her knee while competing in the long jump the summer before she started high school. During her long recovery we often worried about her future, and how the injury would impact her athletic career. But we know God planned her entire life out, which is helping us worry less and trust more, even though we don't know what will happen in her future.

Many times, we question the awful things that happen in our lives, but we have a promise that God is causing everything to eventually work together for our good. This is true when we love God and have answered His call to accept Jesus into our lives. Only then can we trust that anything we experience can be used as a part of God's plan for our life.

Bad things will happen; that's part of living in a sinful world. But we have a guarantee that God will always design good to come from our experiences. When things seem to be going bad, always remember this promise; no matter how long it takes, it will all work out.

WEEK 46

And we know that God causes everything to work together for the good of those who love God and are called according to his purpose for them. (Romans 8:28 NLT)

DAY 1: WARM UP
- ❏ Read this week's verse out loud.
- ❏ Bad things happening to you are a part of life. How do you think something that looks and feels bad can work out for good in your life?
- ❏ Read the scripture out loud again.
- ❏ Pray for God to show you that everything that happens to you can have a purpose.

DAY 2: BREAK IT DOWN
- ❏ Read this week's verse out loud.
- ❏ Rewrite the scripture in your own words and make it personally about you.
- ❏ No matter what you may experience, you learned in Week 17 that God has recorded every day of your life. He has a plan for your life too big for you to understand, which is why faith is so important. How can you have faith in God's plan for your life, even when you can't understand it?
- ❏ Pray that your faith will grow strong enough to accept

what you don't understand.

DAY 3: GET IN POSITION

- ❏ Read this week's verse out loud.
- ❏ You can choose to trust God with your future, even when things are not going well in your present. How can you trust God while dealing with feelings of hopelessness about your current problems?
- ❏ Repeat the scripture out loud.
- ❏ Even when you feel like you have no reason to, ask God to help you trust Him.

DAY 4: HUDDLE UP

- ❏ Read this week's verse out loud.
- ❏ Discuss with your parent, coach, or other trusted adult about a situation they experienced that appeared to be really bad when it happened, but they later realized it eventually worked out good for them. Write down any points or lessons you want to remember.
- ❏ Pray together that you would remember to always be hopeful because things aren't always what they seem.

DAY 5: PUSH THROUGH

- ❏ Try to recite this week's verse out loud without looking.
- ❏ For all things to work together for your good, you must love God. Have you known God for a long time, a short time, or is this book the first time you've heard about Him? Do you love God? How can you grow to love Him?

- ❑ Recite this week's scripture again.
- ❑ End by praying that your relationship with God, and your love for Him, will grow stronger.

DAY 6: PRACTICE MAKES PERFECT

- ❑ Try again to recite this week's verse out loud. Spend time practicing until you can almost say it from memory.
- ❑ The second condition for all things working out for your good is that you must be called for God's purpose in your life. This means you must be committed to living your life in a way that honors Him and obeys His Word. Are you willing to give up the plans you have for your life, and accept God's plans instead? Write down some goals that you have for your life. Put a check mark next to any of them that you are willing to give up for God.
- ❑ Pray that you would trust God's plan for your life over your plans.

DAY 7: FINISH STRONG

- ❑ Recite this week's verse. Spend time practicing until you can say it from memory.
- ❑ Sometimes you may wonder if you messed up your life by making a poor choice or decision, or by something unexpected you experienced. But no matter what has happened, this week's promise tells you that all the things you have experienced, or will experience, will all work together for your good as part of God's plan for your life.

Write down some things that have happened to you that don't seem good now.

❏ Pray that you wouldn't focus on how things appear now, but you would look to the future instead and trust that God will work everything on your list for your good.

❏ Close out this week by saying the scripture from memory.

MIND-BLOWING

Now to him who is able to do **immeasurably** more than all we ask or imagine, according to his power that is at work within us. (Ephesians 3:20 NIV)

This final promise was a popular benediction when I was a child. It would be spoken over the people at the end of the church service. A benediction is a prayer, usually taken from the Bible, spoken as a blessing. It's like saying goodbye in a special way.

This blessing is the promise that God can exceed your every prayer request, wish, and hope. Over this past year, you answered questions each week and wrote down prayers, hopes, and dreams for your life. God can answer whatever you noted and prayed for during your daily workouts, but He can also go above and beyond that. In fact, He's able to do more than you could ever imagine!

> **WORD FOCUS:**
>
> **immeasurably** – not able to be counted or measured

As you finish your journey through this section, you have the foundation to live an amazing life for God. At times it may not be easy, and you will definitely face some challenges, but remember you have all the power you need through the Holy

Spirit, who will work inside of you if you allow Him to. And if you do, your life will never be the same again.

WEEK 47

Now to him who is able to do immeasurably more than all we ask or imagine, according to his power that is at work within us.
(Ephesians 3:20 NIV)

DAY 1: WARM UP
❑ Read this week's verse out loud.
❑ By starting this scripture with "now unto him", it is pointing our attention to God. After all you've learned about God, do you believe there is any limit to what He can do?
❑ Read the scripture out loud again.
❑ Pray that there will never be any limits to what you believe God can do.

DAY 2: BREAK IT DOWN
❑ Read this week's verse out loud.
❑ Rewrite the scripture in your own words and make it personally about you.
❑ God can do more than you can dream, so much more that it can't even be measured by the human mind. Think about

the love God has for you and imagine that it is also too great to describe. How do you think someone that loves you that much will treat you?

❑ Pray that God will help you realize the greatness of the love He has for you.

DAY 3: GET IN POSITION

❑ Read this week's verse out loud.

❑ This promise is only possible through the power of God at work inside of you. You've learned about this power that is given to you by the Holy Spirit. This power is supernatural, which means it's not from this world. God's power is not bound by the rules of this world, so He's able to do more than your mind can understand. Is there anything you want, but don't think is possible for your life?

❑ Repeat the scripture out loud.

❑ Pray that God will open your mind to believe that anything is possible through His power inside of you.

DAY 4: HUDDLE UP

❑ Read this week's verse out loud.

❑ Ask your parent, coach, or other trusted adult to share a story from the Bible that showed God's limitless power. Discuss what happened and how God's power was shown in the situation. What are some points from the story you can write down to remind you of God's power the next time you are struggling to trust Him?

❑ Pray together that as you continue to read the Bible, you will learn more about God's power, so you can trust Him to also do great things for you.

DAY 5: PUSH THROUGH

❑ Try to recite this week's verse out loud without looking.

❑ Another popular translation of this scripture states God can do "exceeding and abundantly more" than you could ask or think. Is there anything you want, that you feel might be too big or too much to ask God for? What is stopping you from asking for what you want?

❑ Recite this week's scripture again.

❑ Pray that you would have the confidence to ask God for what your heart desires.

DAY 6: PRACTICE MAKES PERFECT

❑ Try again to recite this week's verse out loud. Spend time practicing until you can almost say it from memory.

❑ There's no limit to what you can do for God, and for others. If you can dream it, think it, and imagine it, then you should ask for it. But you must also remember what you learned in Week 35 about how you get the desires of your heart. In what ways have you been delighting yourself in God?

❑ Pray that you will continue to delight in God so that He can bless your dreams even more than you can ever imagine.

DAY 7: FINISH STRONG

❑ Recite this week's verse. Spend time practicing until you

can say it from memory.

❑ As you close out the final workout of this section, take this week's benediction with you always. You have had an amazing time of study, growth, and knowledge of God's Playbook to guide you for the rest of your life. It's time to put everything you've learned into action. Finish this workout with your prayer of praise to God in your notes. Now unto Him...

❑ Thank God for all the lessons you learned throughout this book. Ask Him to show you what your next step should be to learn more about Him.

❑ Close out this week by saying the scripture from memory.

Section 8:
USING YOUR PLAYBOOK

WISE UP

Wise choices will watch over you. Understanding will keep you safe.
(Proverbs 2:11 NLT)

One day, you will begin making all your own decisions in life. Your parents won't have any say in what you do, how long you practice, what team you play for, where you go, or what you spend your money on. Do you feel confident that you can make good choices that will affect your future?

Proverbs is considered the book of **wisdom** in the Bible. Wisdom is an invaluable gift that will benefit you in so many ways for the rest of your life. Wisdom brings good judgment and decision-making skills, which can keep you from making bad choices, living with regret, and bringing harm to yourself.

You have learned and discovered so much about God's Word over this past year and now have the knowledge needed to stay on the right path for the rest of your life. However, you will need to use this

> **WORD FOCUS:**
>
> **wisdom** – ability to use knowledge to make good decisions

knowledge to make wise choices. You have gained understanding about what God's Word says about the decisions you should be making throughout your life. Wisdom will show you when and how to make the best choices.

WEEK 48

Wise choices will watch over you. Understanding will keep you safe.
(Proverbs 2:11 NLT)

DAY 1: WARM UP

- ❑ Read this week's verse out loud.
- ❑ Do you feel like you have good knowledge of the Bible? Have you ever used it before to make a decision about your life?
- ❑ Read the scripture out loud again.
- ❑ Pray that God will teach you about wisdom this week.

DAY 2: BREAK IT DOWN

- ❑ Read this week's verse out loud.
- ❑ Rewrite the scripture in your own words and make it personally about you.
- ❑ Think about a poor choice you made recently and write about the negative result you had to face. Was there a better choice you could have made for a different result?
- ❑ Finish your workout asking God for wisdom to make better choices.

Day 3: GET IN POSITION

- ❏ Read this week's verse out loud.
- ❏ How does this message relate to your life right now? How can following this scripture impact your life in the future?
- ❏ Repeat the scripture out loud.
- ❏ End today's workout by praying that God will show you how wisdom and understanding can affect your future.

DAY 4: HUDDLE UP

- ❏ Read this week's verse out loud.
- ❏ Share this week's scripture with your parent, coach, or other trusted adult and discuss a particular situation in which you need support and wisdom to make a decision.
- ❏ Pray together that you will make a wise decision.

DAY 5: PUSH THROUGH

- ❏ Try to recite this week's verse out loud without looking.
- ❏ Determine and write down the choice you want to make for the dilemma you shared yesterday.
- ❏ Recite this week's scripture again.
- ❏ End by praying for courage to follow through on the action you plan to take.

DAY 6: PRACTICE MAKES PERFECT

- ❏ Try again to recite this week's verse out loud. Spend time practicing until you can almost say it from memory.
- ❏ What led you to the decision you made yesterday? What

are the possible outcomes of the choice you want to make?

❑ Pray for wisdom from God, and decide when you are going to act on your choice.

DAY 7: FINISH STRONG

❑ Recite this week's verse. Spend time practicing until you can say it from memory.

❑ Decide on when and how you are going to act on your decision. Write your plan down and be sure to note what happened as a result.

❑ Pray that God always helps you remember to make wise choices, and close out this week by saying your scripture from memory.

LIGHT IT UP

Your word is a lamp to guide my feet and a light for my path.

(Psalm 119:105 NLT)

Have you ever been in the pitch black, not able to see anything but darkness? When I was younger, my family visited Crystal Cave in Kutztown, Pennsylvania. When we were deep into the cave, the guide turned the lights off and asked us to move our hands in front of our eyes. No matter how hard I tried, I couldn't see anything!

This week's strategy informs us that the Bible is the light we need to guide the path in our life. Each week as you read, studied, and learned the Word of God, it was lighting up your pathway. When you feel comfortable enough to make a decision on your own, always look to the Word of God to keep you going in the right direction.

In life, there are many decisions you will need to make. Some may be quick—like what move to make or play to run during an important game, and others may have a long-term impact—like which friends to choose, what college to attend, or what career path to follow. The Bible is your playbook and guide to light your way. Always use it so you never have to be lost in the dark.

WEEK 49

Your word is a lamp to guide my feet and a light for my path.
(Psalm 119:105 NLT)

DAY 1: WARM UP

❑ Read this week's verse out loud.

❑ Imagine waking up in a completely dark, unknown place. What would you do to find your way out?

❑ Read the scripture out loud again.

❑ Pray for God to speak to you about finding direction for your life this week.

DAY 2: BREAK IT DOWN

❑ Read this week's verse out loud.

❑ Rewrite the scripture in your own words, making it personally about you.

❑ How does this message relate to your life right now? How can it impact your future?

❑ Pray that God will show you how He can guide your life.

DAY 3: GET IN POSITION

❑ Read this week's verse out loud.

❑ Is there a decision about your future that you're not sure about? How does this scripture help you determine what to do next?

- ❏ Repeat the scripture out loud.
- ❏ Ask God for help in deciding what choice you should make.

DAY 4: HUDDLE UP

- ❏ Read this week's verse out loud.
- ❏ Share this week's scripture with your parent, coach, or other trusted adult, discuss your decision from yesterday, and ask for guidance and direction on the next steps you should take.
- ❏ Pray together that you will stay on God's path for your life.

DAY 5: PUSH THROUGH

- ❏ Try to recite this week's verse out loud without looking.
- ❏ How can you commit to using God's Word as a guide for your life? Have you found direction for the decision you need to make for your future?
- ❏ Recite this week's scripture again.
- ❏ End by praying that you will understand what you read in the Bible.

DAY 6: PRACTICE MAKES PERFECT

- ❏ Try again to recite this week's verse out loud. Spend time practicing until you can almost say it from memory.
- ❏ Are you confident you will know how to use God's Word when you face a tough decision in the future?
- ❏ Pray for understanding of God's Word as you read it.

DAY 7: FINISH STRONG

- ❑ Recite this week's verse. Spend time practicing until you can say it from memory.
- ❑ Write down how you use the Word of God when you need to make a decision in the future.
- ❑ Thank God for the direction He has given you this week.
- ❑ Close out this week by saying the scripture from memory.

Born This Way

All of us have sinned and fallen short of God's glory.

(Romans 3:23 CEV)

In the Garden of Eden, Adam made a choice to disobey God. He was told not to eat fruit from a certain tree, but he did it anyway. As a result, all humans that came after him were stuck with a life of sin. It's like we all **inherited** sinful **DNA**, and there's nothing we can do to get rid of it.

No matter how hard we try to live a perfect life, we will never be able to. The sin in our lives separates us from God because we fail to meet His standard for living. There is no way you can ever be perfect due to your sinful nature.

WORD FOCUS:

inherit – to receive something from someone else, usually a family member

DNA – information found in the human body that determines how a person grows and develops

People may sometimes try to judge different levels of sin, like saying a little white lie isn't too bad, or that murder is one of the worst sins ever. But no matter what it is, all sin offends God. We are all guilty of being sinners and need to be saved from it. As you learned in this book, God came up with an amazing plan to save us, and His playbook helps us live the best way that we can.

WEEK 50

All of us have sinned and fallen short of God's glory.

(Romans 3:23 CEV)

DAY 1: WARM UP

❑ Read this week's verse out loud.

❑ What do you think it means to be a sinner? How does it make you feel to know you are a sinner?

❑ Read the scripture out loud again.

❑ Pray for God to speak to you this week about the sin in your life, and what you can do about it.

DAY 2: BREAK IT DOWN

❑ Read this week's verse out loud.

❑ Rewrite the scripture in your own words and make it personally about you.

❑ How do you know what sin is? Is there anything you have read before that explains sin? Have your parents or guardians raised you to know right from wrong? Explain how.

❑ Finish your workout by praying that God will show you

any sin in your life.

DAY 3: GET IN POSITION

❏ Read this week's verse out loud.
❏ What do you think you can do to avoid sin in your life? Do you ever feel something inside of you warning you not to do certain things? What do you think that is, and what should you do when you feel it?
❏ Repeat the scripture out loud.
❏ Ask God to help you feel when He warns you from doing something you shouldn't, and to respond correctly to the warning.

DAY 4: HUDDLE UP

❏ Read this week's verse out loud.
❏ Share this week's scripture with your parent, coach, or other trusted adult and discuss the sin that may be in your life. Discuss the importance of obeying the trusted adults in your life since disobedience or doing something you know—or were told—not to do, always leads to sin.
❏ Pray together that God will help you obey those in authority over you.

DAY 5: PUSH THROUGH

❏ Try to recite this week's verse out loud without looking.
❏ To keep from sinning, you must also follow the law of your government, the rules of your school, and policies for your sport. Write how you can follow all the rules around you.

- ❑ Recite this week's scripture again.
- ❑ End by praying that God will help you follow the rules to the best of your ability.

DAY 6: PRACTICE MAKES PERFECT

- ❑ Try again to recite this week's verse out loud. Spend time practicing until you can almost say it from memory.
- ❑ Seek the help of others, along with God's help. What can you do to be aware of the temptation to sin?
- ❑ Pray that God will help you respond correctly when you are tempted to sin.

DAY 7: FINISH STRONG

- ❑ Recite this week's verse. Spend time practicing until you can say it from memory.
- ❑ This week was focused on the sin in your life, but you don't have to handle it on your own. In Week 6, you learned one of the most important scriptures in the Bible. It was about God's plan to beat the sin in your life. Have you made a decision to accept Jesus into your life? If not, is there something holding you back?
- ❑ Pray that God will help you learn how to keep sin out of your life, so you are not separated from Him.
- ❑ Close out this week by saying the scripture from memory.

DEEP DOWN INSIDE

I have hidden your word in my heart that I might not sin against you. (Psalm 119:11 NIV)

The Pixar movie *Inside Out* took place in the mind of a pre-teen girl named Riley. When Riley went to sleep at night, her brain transferred what she'd seen and learned that day to her **long-term memory**. There were memories stored from when she was much younger that she still remembered. Some included happier times, while others were sad or painful. But both good and bad memories helped her make choices in the movie.

Each week, as you reviewed the same verse for seven days, you practiced and created memories of what you've read. This helped hide the words and message deep into your heart and mind for future use, which will help you make good choices instead of sinful ones.

While practicing your sport, you must repeat new skills until they are in your long-term memory, and you can perform them without having to think about it. As you continue to

> **WORD FOCUS:**
>
> **long-term memory** – information that can be remembered over a long period of time

read the Bible, you will learn spiritual lessons and skills to use so you're not confused about which decision to make. As scriptures switch to your long-term memory, you'll be able to pull them up anytime you need them, to help you make good choices for the rest of your life.

WEEK 51

I have hidden your word in my heart that I might not sin against you. (Psalm 119: 11 NIV)

DAY 1: WARM UP

❑ Read this week's verse out loud.
❑ What kind of things have you hidden in your mind—songs, memories, or something you've watched? Have they been helping or hurting you?
❑ Read the scripture out loud again.
❑ Pray for God to speak to you this week about being aware of what you allow in your mind.

DAY 2: BREAK IT DOWN

❑ Read this week's verse out loud.
❑ Rewrite the scripture in your own words and make it personally about you.

- Completing each day's workout, prepares the weekly scripture for your long-term memory. How do you think this will affect your future?
- Finish your workout by praying for understanding of what your mind learns each day.

DAY 3: GET IN POSITION

- Read this week's verse out loud.
- Think of something you did recently without thinking, that had a negative outcome. Maybe it was something you said or a reaction on the field or court. How can you make better choices in a split moment?
- Repeat the scripture out loud.
- Ask God for help in knowing how to respond better to tough situations based on His Word.

DAY 4: HUDDLE UP

- Read this week's verse out loud.
- Share this week's scripture with your parent, coach, or other trusted adult and discuss changes you can make that will lead to better choices, based on the scriptures you've read and learned throughout this devotional.
- Pray together that God helps you turn off any sources of information that do not benefit you.

DAY 5: PUSH THROUGH

- Try to recite this week's verse out loud without looking.
- Think about all the information you have in your long-

term memory. How does the Word of God fit on the level of importance to everything else you know?

❑ Recite this week's scripture again.

❑ End by praying that God will help you understand what information is most important for you to know.

DAY 6: PRACTICE MAKES PERFECT

❑ Try again to recite this week's verse out loud. Spend time practicing until you can almost say it from memory.

❑ Think about a difficult skill you had to learn for your sport. How long did you practice it until you could perform it in a game without having to think about it? How can you apply that to this week's lesson?

❑ Pray that you will continue to memorize God's Word to help you make the best choices.

DAY 7: FINISH STRONG

❑ Recite this week's verse. Spend time practicing until you can say it from memory.

❑ Decide to hide God's Word to help you throughout your life. Write down the steps you will take to use His Word to make good choices in the future.

❑ Pray that God helps you remember how important this scripture is for making future choices.

❑ Close out this week by saying the scripture from memory.

THE REAL SECRET TO SUCCESS

Study this Book of Instruction continually. Meditate on it day and night so you will be sure to obey everything written in it. Only then will you prosper and succeed in all you do.

(Joshua 1:8 NLT)

What if I told you I had the answer for you to always be a winner or to have *success* in whatever you do? Would you believe me? Many books, tips, and suggestions have been given about how to be successful. Luckily, you don't have to worry about any of that, because this week's strategy clearly defines what you need to do to experience success.

The first step is to study the Book of Instruction, which is the Bible, repeatedly. You started this step by reading this devotional. Continue to do this as you grow older. The next step is to *meditate* on it day and night. The workouts you completed each day helped you meditate and think about what you were reading and how to apply it to your life.

The final step is to

WORD FOCUS:

success – having completed a goal, usually by working hard for it

meditate – think deeply about something

obey everything written in it. This is the tough part, as not everything you read will be easy to do. First, you must decide if you want to be successful or not. You will always have directions for making good choices and decisions, but you can't decide to only obey certain things while ignoring other stuff you've read in the Bible. This is an all-or-nothing deal for success. If you choose to follow this plan for success, it won't be easy, but it will definitely be worth it

WEEK 52

Study this Book of Instruction continually. Meditate on it day and night so you will be sure to obey everything written in it. Only then will you prosper and succeed in all you do.

(Joshua 1:8 NLT)

DAY 1: WARM UP

❑   Read this week's verse out loud.
❑   Write down your definition of success. Write down what you have been doing to be successful.
❑   Read the scripture out loud again.
❑   Pray for God to speak to you this week about the changes you need to make to be successful.

DAY 2: BREAK IT DOWN

- ❑ Read this week's verse out loud.
- ❑ Rewrite the scripture in your own words and make it personally about you.
- ❑ Review each step for success. Write down how you think each step will help you be successful.
- ❑ Finish today's workout with a prayer to better understand each step for success.

DAY 3: GET IN POSITION

- ❑ Read this week's verse out loud.
- ❑ Have you decided to follow the steps? Do you think it will be tough to follow any of the steps? If so, why?
- ❑ Repeat the scripture out loud.
- ❑ Ask God for help in understanding the purpose of the steps to success found in this week's scripture.

DAY 4: HUDDLE UP

- ❑ Read this week's verse out loud.
- ❑ Share this week's scripture with your parent, coach, or other trusted adult and discuss the steps to success. Ask if they have any suggestions for other ways to study the Bible, including other devotionals, Bible guides, or reading plans.
- ❑ Pray together for direction in applying the steps for success to your life.

DAY 5: PUSH THROUGH

❏ Try to recite this week's verse out loud without looking.

❏ What is the best way for you to follow the steps with everything going on in your life? Decide on what you will commit to do to be successful.

❏ Recite this week's scripture again.

❏ End by praying for help with making any changes needed in your life to help you follow the steps for success.

DAY 6: PRACTICE MAKES PERFECT

❏ Try again to recite this week's verse out loud. Spend time practicing until you can almost say it from memory.

❏ According to the 1st step, you must study the Word of God continually. Write down what kind of study schedule you will try to maintain after you finish this devotional.

❏ Pray that God shows you how to include the rules in your daily schedule.

DAY 7: FINISH STRONG

❏ Recite this week's verse. Spend time practicing until you can say it from memory.

❏ Decide to follow the steps to success given to Joshua after he became the new leader of God's people. Write down three areas you want to have success in before you finish this devotional, and how following the steps will help you achieve your goals.

❏ Pray that God helps you follow the steps to success as you work to achieve your goals.

❑ Close out this week by saying the scripture from memory.

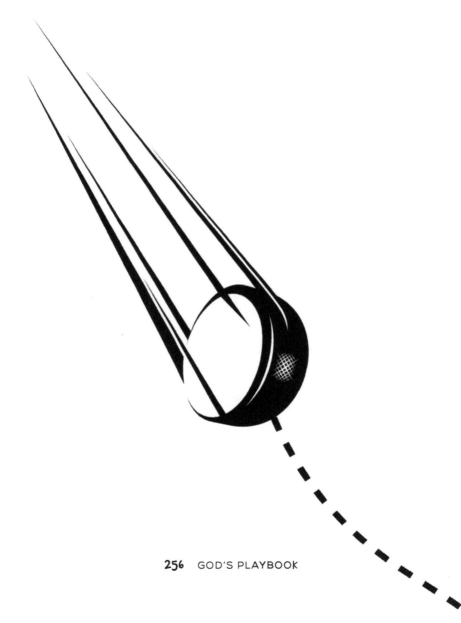

AFTERWORD

Congratulations on finishing this book! It may have taken a year, or for some of you, a bit longer. It doesn't matter, as long as you finished!

I wanted to take this opportunity to give anyone who has never asked Jesus to be their Lord and Savior a chance to do so. God's Playbook is only effective for those that believe in His Son, Jesus. Remember what you learned in Week 6? I know it was almost a year ago, so take the time to go back and read it if you need to.

If you are ready to invite Jesus into your life, please pray these words out loud:

DEAR JESUS,
THANK YOU FOR COMING TO EARTH
AND DYING ON THE CROSS FOR MY
SINS. I BELIEVE YOU ROSE FROM YOUR
GRAVE ON THE THIRD DAY AND NOW
LIVE IN HEAVEN. PLEASE COME INTO
MY LIFE AND FORGIVE ME OF MY
SINS. I RECEIVE YOU AS MY PERSONAL
SAVIOR AND LORD. PLEASE TEACH ME
HOW TO LIVE FOR YOU.
IN YOUR NAME I PRAY, AMEN.

If you prayed those words, I want to be the first to congratulate you on this life-changing decision and welcome you to God's family.

Please let your parent, coach, or another trusted person know about your decision, so that they can celebrate with you, and also support you as this is the most important choice you have ever made.

If you're not ready to make this decision yet, it's okay. Keep reading the Bible to learn more about God, and I will be praying that He speaks to your heart. If you should change your mind, feel free to come back here any time and say this prayer out loud.

ACKNOWLEDGEMENT

THANK YOU!

God – the Father, the Son, and the Holy Spirit. It is in honor of you and for your glory that I write.

Kenny for your steadfast love, support, and commitment.

Kennedi and Kassadi – You are my pride and joy and the reason for this book. Always keep God's word deep in your heart.

Mom and Dad for teaching me the Word of God at a very young age and investing time to make sure I learned every memory verse.

To my extended family for your unwavering support of my work.

Remy for always watching over my words.

Destined 4 the Dub and Faith-Filled Moms community for your encouragement and for reading every blog.

Victory in Christ Christian Center and my IPT (you know who you are) for keeping me lifted in prayer.

Publishing in Color for getting me started on my writing career.

Taneki and Vine Publishing for your patience, guidance, and vision in birthing my first book - my baby!

To those I failed to mention by name, but who still deserve gratitude.

CPSIA information can be obtained
at www.ICGtesting.com
Printed in the USA
JSHW062328070123
35823JS00004B/5

9 781736 748398